BLOCKCHAIN
The decentralized revolution

1MillionXbtc

ISBN: 9781679348730

ABOUT US

The objective of creating quality training content on cryptocurrencies and blockchain has joined a group of passionate users of the "Internet of Value" and decentralized models under the name of 1Millionxbtc, which express their conviction in the promising future of the Bitcoin and blockchain technology.

On this occasion, we have made a manual to understand blockchain technology, called to revolutionize the internet and the means on which bitcoin is based. This technology will change the internet and the world as we know it for its technical and social possibilities.

For any questions, you can email us to **1millionxbtc@gmail.com**.

Regards.

1 Million X btc

1Millionxbtc

CONTENT

FOREWORD

Dear Luis:

I email you normal 'cause I know you're

No able to email like every one of our friends have

done for almost 30 years. So bad that all this time you never

wanted to know what Internet has become, emails, e-commerce,

credit cards, music downloads and movies for personal rejoicing,

smartphones with or without Cameras, personal security in the p2p

environment with 2fa and overall, every other wonders like social media

that cover our lives with double or even, triple existence. Taking part in the

Mind Capital platform which flag is the transparency based on blockchain

This new experience is affecting me so, that I notice I'm speaking different

Grouping the words that pile themselves and I'm surprised to see that writing

also get another new form. It's like if lines and paragraphs take on the blockchain

appearance. I think modernity is getting too deep inside me that it's changing me.

It must be truth when they say that blockchain will be as revolutionary as internet

nowadays. I see you're not so up to date with these topic, so I send you this

little book for you to learn more about what's happening now.

Please, read it carefully, my dearest.

Dolores, your forever girlfriend

(Gonzalo García Pelayo)

1Millionxbtc

WHAT IS BLOCKCHAIN?

The internet revolution

The clearest way to describe blockchain would be to say that it is just a new technology that has come to revolutionize the internet and its operation. Blockchain is able to affect virtually our entire environment by changing the way we understand the world.

Blockchain turns the internet of information into an internet of value, revolutionizing the concept of digital applications and creating a freer and safer world. It is about the absolute connection between users, without intermediaries: the freedom of two people to be able to act at opposite ends of the planet under the conditions that only they stipulate, without anyone else having access to that pact and giving power to people in instead of organizations or platforms.

This technology is being key to the arrival of a new digital revolution called to be as spectacular as was the birth of the internet itself. To get an idea: the birth of the internet allowed us to receive information, obtain it through consultations in a unidirectional process. We, as users, were simple recipients who accessed the information that a server could or wanted to offer us.

At present, interactivity has increased: we not only receive information, we are not just receivers, but we also transmit it by generating small networks. For example, when you interact in a certain social network by uploading photos or sending messages, you can share your actions with its members in a two-way direction. The limitation is that it is always done through an intermediary platform, so that everything you do is registered on its servers and is accessible to its owners. You cannot interact without someone else in between who could, at any time, manipulate, use or access your information. You are always in the hands of that "supervisor."

But in the future, with the implementation of Blockchain, the interactivity will be absolute and independent. The exchange of information will stop focusing on small cores or platforms to become global. It will allow to turn the internet into a great global brain. For example: imagine that you are looking for certain information in the Google search engine. You will only get pages that are indexed in that search engine that, no matter how good it is, in addition to not incorporating all the internet, you can register your searches and decide what it shows and what does not, depending on your own interests; that is, what is the most beneficial for you, economically. Your access to information will always depend ultimately on them. Instead, blockchain technology would allow the incorporation of information on a global scale, without limits and without control, as if it were a universal search engine capable of containing all the information in the world without anyone being able to control it. An information store as it is, not as someone decides what it should be.

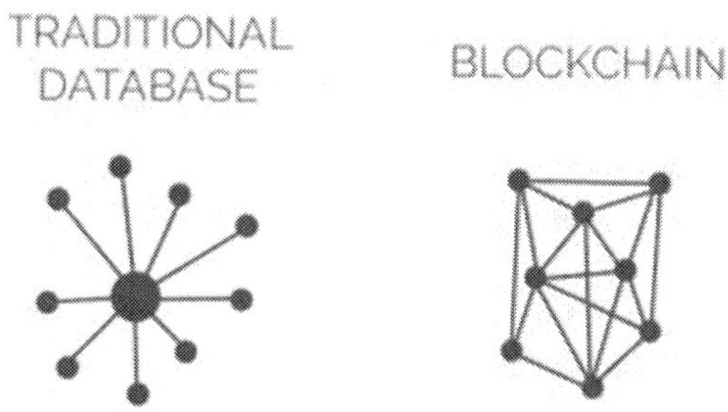

IceGold chart that shows the difference between the current information transfers that requires a centralizing core or server with its own limitations and the Blockchain effect that allows the free distribution of information in a wider global system

This freedom of exchange eliminates censorship and allows individual connection without outside observers. Imagine living with someone in your house supervising all your actions, from the most routine to the most intimate. That is the internet today. Blockchain will eliminate that observer, that snoop, which will expand the capacity of connections to infinity.

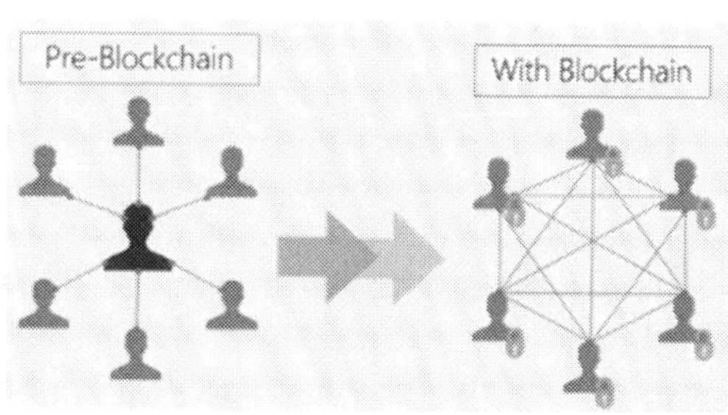

This Steemit scheme clearly shows how a third-party third party is currently required to connect two users and with blockchain two users will be able to transfer information without the presence of this one.

Practical exercise 1

In this exercise, we will practice how the exchange of information in the blockchain works. Below are two schemes that represent different information flows. Associate each of them with each of the statements under the representation:

A) It is a traditional database, since all the information comes from the same centralized server and there can be no direct exchange between users.

B) It is a blockchain since there is no centralizing element and all users can share information freely

However, before understanding its influence on society and functionalities, it is convenient to know this technology from a closer objective and technical point of view to really know what makes this digital revolution allow.

A blockchain is nothing more than a database distributed among different users, cryptographically protected in which transactions and exchanges are added in the form of blocks one after another, so that the history of its activity is stored from the beginning until the present moment of driving safe and secret thanks to the encryption.

This information store belongs to nobody and at the same time belongs to everyone. It is not located on a single master server, but appears on multiple computers that act on it. The blockchain is replicated in the devices of its users, so that none of them has the power to modify it or establish a functioning at will because it would be "supervised" by the rest. This chain is copied in each transaction, and always responding to that immovable historical record that prevents it from being manipulated. A change in a single chain that is not validated and incorporated in the rest would not be effective. Or all, or none. That is to say: the blockchain is a database on which everyone can act, but in which no one has the ability to handle it to their interest since all their copies have to be synchronized and it is impossible to manipulate them all at once.

Imagine that you are the treasurer of a group of friends and that you are in charge of managing its economy. In your account book you write down each entry and exit of money and every week, you give a copy to each member of the economic movements to keep them informed. As you are the only manager, you could manipulate your notebook as you wish and the group would only be informed each time you give them the periodic copy. Therefore, throughout the week you could manipulate the accounts, because members only have that weekly reference.

Instead, imagine that at each entry and exit of money to the group, even if it was a cent of a euro, you had to make a copy of the accounts and inform the members and that, in addition, they compared the information received to verify that they all coincide and that also match all previous records. Each variation would be subject to a thorough examination and it would be impossible to manipulate the accounts. That is what the blockchain does regarding the data it manages.

Blockchains are decentralized databases. They do not depend on a manager or entity that regulates them and can alter their operation. They follow rules established by and for the group. Rules that act without the need for an intermediary, without bias or exceptions.

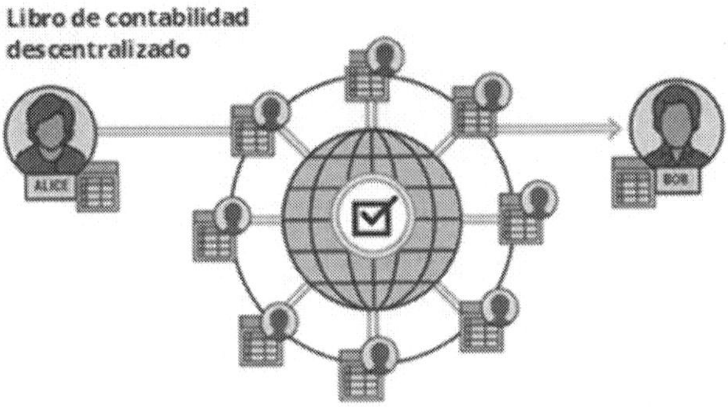

As this RankiaPro scheme shows, Blockchain is an account book shared by all its users that automatically verifies that the changes noted in each user's book matches that of all others.

Every centralized database in which our information must necessarily pass through an intermediary entity requires trust that is not always absolute. Blockchain ends that uncertainty and that need to surrender to a stranger. The exchanges in the blockchain are anonymous and will be carried out, yes or yes, under the characteristics with which this chain works, without anyone being able to alter them.

This 100% trust that Blockchain provides when eliminating the intermediary is key to understanding its potential for involvement in society. Can you imagine being able to exchange information without having to go through a server where it can be intercepted? Or exchange money without a financial entity setting limits of amount, geographic or legal? It is the end of the limiting regulations. Absolute freedom

We will see later what applications and uses can benefit from this system of total anonymity and absolute confidence and why Blockchain is called to revolutionize the internet.

These chains can have free access allowing any user (public blockchain) to use them or they can limit their access to a specific group of people (private blockchain). The latter are effective for small groups or groups in particular that want to regulate the exchanges between them without anyone else being able to access their database.

In addition to that, chains can also differ in any of their characteristics. A blockchain can be designed with certain functionalities depending on where it will be implanted and the use that will be given. That is, each blockchain can work in a different way from another. But as we said, once it is developed and implemented, all its users play under the same rules.

In short: what makes Blockchain so special and will allow such an impressive digital revolution?

- *Huge databases*: block chains allow you to establish databases globally. Currently, all the information is stored in concrete bases and delimited by its own size. For example, a user who only uses Google will only be able to access the information indexed in that search engine. Or an Instagram user, you can only contact through this application with other users of that same social network. However, Blockchain-based databases can have global scalability, so that it is capable of containing all the global information. The clearest example is Bitcoin, a network that reaches every corner of the world and every user that participates with this currency.

- *Immutable information*: the conditions on which a particular block chain operates cannot be changed, they are established in their programming and are obeyed without the possibility of breaking their own rules. Users establish rules of participation in its creation and these cannot be altered. If we follow the example of bitcoin, this makes it work in a way and that no one, at any given time, can change its characteristics. This allows consensus and 100% confidence, since there is no supervisor who can change the rules of the game at will.

- *Immovable registration*: all activity around a blockchain is recorded from its inception until today. Everything that is done is incorporated, and it must also be in accordance with the rest of the existing blockchain copies in each of the nodes that access it. This prevents individual traps from being established, since any change is contrasted with other users. This avoids any type of manipulation since as the entire chain is preserved, there are always as many references as copies of it so that it is not altered.

- *Decentralization*: there is no central unit through which you have to pass all the information or that can change the operation. This allows absolute confidentiality and freedom of exchange between users. Although the activities are registered and agreed by all the nodes, the process is carried out in an encrypted manner, so that only those interested in the exchange are aware of it.

THE BLOCKCHAIN TECHNOLOGY

Bitcoin and Blockchain

Bitcoin and blockchain are two terms that are often associated interchangeably, and that even many people treat as two sides of the same coin. Bitcoin is made use of blockchain technology, but they are not the same thing at all. Currency is an application created through the use of blockchain technology. In fact, it was the first to use it and the one that has become more popular, hence that association. So, to really understand what blockchain means and its true potential, it is imperative to understand cryptocurrency and how it made blockchain technology a reality.

Bitcoin and the First Use of Blockchain

In the 1990s, a group of netizens began to dream of an open, free, anonymous, transparent financial system and without the need for banking entities or intermediaries to which one had to resort necessarily to use their money. Why did there always have to be someone sticking their hands in their coins to use them?

This idea finally materialized in 2008 with the launch of bitcoin, a cryptocurrency that could be exchanged between users without having to be issued by any government or controlled by any official organization. Its creator, Satoshi Nakamoto, found in Blockchain the right tool to be able to address all the features he needed this currency to have, thus giving the first use of history to the blockchain.

Thanks to Blockchain, the virtual currency could be exchanged between two opposite ends of the planet in total confidentiality, without the need of the approval of central organizations, through the value that only the two interested parties of the exchange would like to give and without anyone or anything that imposed their conditions on the transaction. Bitcoins are created in a limited and expensive way, so that they manifest the necessary shortage and this makes users give value, necessary characteristics so that they can be used as money. That value, by the way, depends on its users and not on a government that can manipulate it.

But how to ensure that a digital asset cannot be duplicated as any other file? How to make a bitcoin cannot be replicated as is done with a song or a text document? Blockchain put a solution to this problem, since its technology allows a digital file not to be duplicated, so that the same bitcoin cannot exist twice and therefore cannot be copied or pirated. Since bitcoin has a digital character, if it could be duplicated it could not work as a currency. On the other hand, when the blockchain behaves as a register where all activity is incorporated and contrasted under the algorithm of the chain itself, it is possible to give each file a unique identity. By preventing it by its own code and operation, in its rules inscribed in its programming, it avoids by definition the counterfeit of bitcoins, makes it impossible, generating the necessary confidence for its usefulness.

And how does this make it possible? Imagine that in a group of 20 people, 100 bitcoins are distributed, 5 bitcoins per individual, and that all of them have a notebook where they write down how much each one has. If an individual A gave 3 bitcoins to another individual B in exchange for a service, the first individual would have to subtract them from his notebook, and the second, add them. But in addition, the other 18 individuals who have not participated in the exchange, would also note that A has given B those 3 bitcoins, so that the entries of all involved would have to match. That is what blockchain does globally automatically. Update the book of each individual in each exchange even to verify that the exchange is true and not an individual alteration or duplicate, and also does it in an encrypted way so that only A and B are aware of said exchange, even if it has to be agreed and validated by all users. That is the magic of Blockchain.

Simple scheme of queesbitcoin.info that shows how if the same transaction is duplicated, only the one that is validated by the rest of users is accepted in the block chain, rejecting the other.

Practical exercise 2

Determine if the following statements are true or false:

	T	F
Bitcoin is the commercial name of blockchain technology, but deep down they are the same thing		
Bitcoin is a banking entity which objective is to end the rest of the banking entities		
Blockchain is an account record in which each user has a copy of the history		
If the same bitcoin is sent to two different people at the same time each receiver receives one		
The fact that a server verifies all transactions prevents the copy of bitcoins		

The special features of blockchain allowed bitcoin to be used as a means of payment, by making transactions more secure. But now blockchains are no longer only used to operate with bitcoins, many payment platforms also incorporate them to increase their security rates. Blockchain has extended beyond the pioneer currency that saw it born to be incorporated into numerous digital payment platforms, and also in applications so diverse that they have nothing to do with the economy.

Blockchain and the absolute trust of bitcoin

To participate in the Bitcoin network, you only need to download the client and install it on a computer. This can be done by anyone, since it is in the public domain. Once installed, a complete copy of the chain is made on the computer, making it a node capable of operating on it.

At that time, the node maintains a copy of the blockchain exactly the same as that of other users and is updated at the same time as all others. That is, when installing the Bitcoin client, a user acquires one of those "account books" in which all the universal changes that are made on the blockchain are recorded, so that he becomes a supervisor rather than ensures that this works correctly and under the conditions that were programmed.Anyone can become part of the Bitcoin network. No one can deny access to another person. Nor is it necessary to provide personal data for this. It is a free access network, in which all users have the same options to participate on it on equal terms. No one can prevent a transaction between two users because the protocol of the chain itself dictates it. This was something impossible before the implementation of Blockchain. If you wanted to send money to another person, you had to do it through an entity that allowed it under its own rules the transaction (limitation of the amount, currency changes, commissions, troublesome problems ...) and of course after being identified. Blockchain ends these limitations by allowing free exchanges, always on equal terms between users.

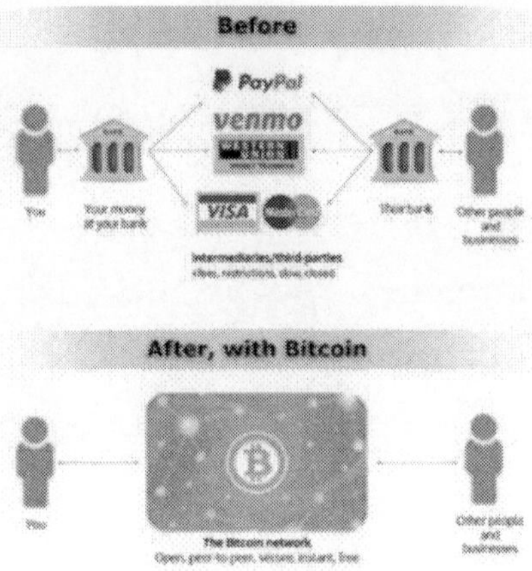

Reddit scheme showing that before bitcoin, an intermediary entity or platform was necessary for any exchange

Practical Exercise 3

Transform the following statements to match with the Bitcoin blockchain:

A) To participate in the Bitcoin blockchain it is necessary to request a prior permit.

B) Once the Bitcoin client is installed, the user obtains an address to access the server where the main chain is located each time he wants to operate on it.

C) The copy of the user's chain is updated every time he makes a transaction.

D) To complete the first transaction you must fill out a form with personal data.

E) A user can veto access to another if he gets the vote of another 1,000 users.

F) Veteran users are better positioned in the chain and have personal advantages.

G) In order for a transaction between users to be carried out, it must be verified by the creator of Bitcoin.

The blockchain cannot be intervened. To change the protocol, and therefore the way it works, it would be necessary to change most of all existing blockchains! And as we have seen, each user can have a copy on their own computer. No one has absolute control over all of them since any user anywhere in the world can become a watchman.

Let's put a practical example: citizens of Brazil, Ecuador, Argentina, Iceland and Cyprus have seen at least once in their history how their financial institutions prevented them from accessing money from their accounts. In the so-called "corralitos" (partial freezing of bank accounts), the bank turned off the tap and prevented customers from accessing their financial resources.

At the moment when the government detects a worrying national economic situation, it can allow (and in fact do) the banks to conserve money by refusing to give it to their owners. To do this, entities only have to manipulate their own software so that cashiers stop providing users with cash by decision exclusively of the entity, regardless of their customers.

If someone tried to do something like that on Blockchain, he would see that the blockchain doesn't even give him the option to make this possible. Any change must be agreed upon by the existence of hundreds of thousands of copies of the chain around the world. No one can close Bitcoin, or prevent access to its users. A chain cannot be imposed on the rest; a specific decision cannot prevail over the rest of the chains. Each copy of the chain is a declaration of intentions, it is a voice next to another shouting "these are the rules that we have all decided and nobody can change them".

Society tends to think of banks as trusted agents, as in entities that protect their money, when they can really do what they want with it. They invest it in products and, in case their bets go wrong, they just have to declare bankruptcy to disregard. They limit the amount of cash we can withdraw daily. They impose their commissions...

It is infinity of actions that make our money not exactly safe with them.

Banks are like, "I'm sorry, I didn't say what I said I said," because they can change their conditions arbitrarily.

In contrast, a Blockchain-based financial system cannot change the conditions for which it was programmed. Knowing the characteristics of the blockchain you can know exactly in what conditions your money will be, because there are no intermediaries that can act beyond the protocol of the chain itself.

Practical exercise 4

Read the following news posted on The vanguard:

"The finance ministers of the euro zone agreed at dawn on Saturday an unprecedented measure, which taxes customers of Cypriot banks with an extraordinary fee to help pay the financial bailout. As a consequence, Cyprus lives the first partial yard of the European Union.

Hundreds of people were trying to take their money from the banks early on Saturday morning, but they had already frozen the corresponding rate.

As reported by the RIK radio, the online system of financial institutions was blocked and shortly thereafter the subsidiaries of cooperative banks (open on Saturdays), to which dozens of customers had gone, closed.

And it is that after the agreement of the ministers, the president of the Eurogroup, Jeroen Dijsselbloem, announced that those who have deposits below 100,000 euros ($ 130,700) will have to contribute to the financial rescue with a rate of 6.75 percent of their savings. This will be 9.9 percent for sums that exceed 100,000 euros. In recent days, all Cypriot banks had ensured that, as in the rest of the EU, deposits had a guarantee of up to 100,000 euros.

"We have been very careful when distributing the load (of the rescue)," said the Dutchman Dijsselbloem. "We are not punishing Cyprus." The aid package for the Mediterranean island will have an amount of up to 10,000 million euros, without which Cyprus was bankrupt. "The Eurogroup has accomplished its mission," French Economy Minister Pierre Moscovici said on Twitter.

Although the country only contributes 0.2 percent of the eurozone's GDP, "Cyprus is relevant to the system," said EU Economic and Monetary Affairs Commissioner Olli Rehn. This means that the bankruptcy of Cyprus would damage the entire euro zone. The aid package, which has yet to be ratified by several parliaments of the Member States, will be effective in the second half of April.

According to the ministers, the fee imposed on savers will have a unique character and is an exceptional measure. It will affect both Cypriot clients and foreigners with accounts in the country, who could not do anything to prevent it. "Before the banks open, the corresponding amount will have been frozen. The rest of the money will be available," said Jörg Asmussen, a member of the Executive Committee of the European Central Bank.

A) The financial system of Cyprus decided in 2013, in addition to preventing bank customers from withdrawing their money, that a percentage of those savings would be taken to pay the European bailout. Do you think it would be possible to do something like that with bitcoins?

Bitcoin transactions

If we try to understand the operation of Bitcoin in a much clearer and more precise way, we should understand how each of its transactions works. Imagine a novice user who installs his Bitcoin client on his computer. The first thing this does is download a full copy of the chain, and the user becomes one more member of the chain: he already has his account book to participate in this community consensus.

This user will receive a bitcoin payment from another user who will make a payment. To do this, the issuer has to access its own portfolio. A portfolio is a reference address in the blockchain where its assets are located. To move them from one address to another, a digital signature is required that is done through a private key. Therefore, the issuing user accesses its portfolio, verifies that it has funds to make the transaction and authorizes it through its private key. The use of this key is what verifies that the new user of those funds will be the receiving user.

In order for the receiving user to finally receive the funds, this operation must be validated by the miners. The activity of these network workers causes the transaction to be confirmed, as arbitrators, and included as a block in the blockchain. Once verified, the receiving user can now have the funds transferred.

Blockchain components

What are the components that make Blockchain technology exist? What are the parts on which it is based? What would we find if we tried to tear apart a blockchain in order to understand how it works? The truth is that despite the technical complexity of the chain, it is not divided into large parts since its true reason for being is the connection between its users, and therefore makes these its main elements, transforming them into nodes.

Nodes are the access points to the blockchain through which information can be obtained and communicated with it. They are the elements that interact with the chain. They are usually physical elements such as a computer, although virtual nodes may exist. All nodes must share the same software and protocol, that is, they have to use the same digital language so that the transfer of information can be effective. If they are in charge of interacting with the chain, they have to know how to read it and be able to send messages, and for that they must use a common communication protocol.

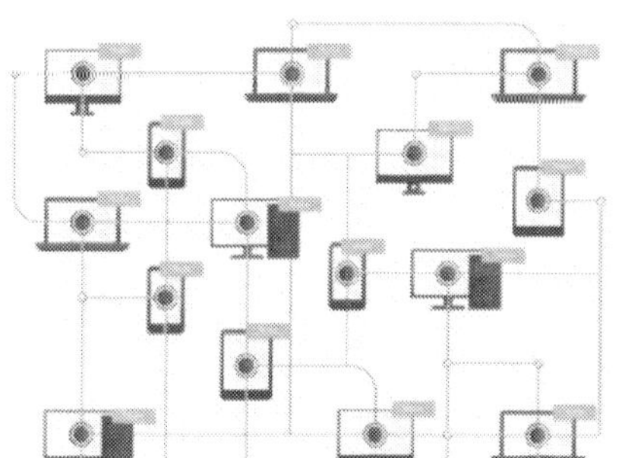

Each node is simply a connected device that operates on blockchain as this Lisk illustration shows

These nodes connect through a P2P (peer-to-peer) network, in which communication is direct between them. In this network formed by all P2P connections there is no established order. All nodes have the same importance and power. It does not happen as in centralized systems, where all the information has to pass through a higher element so that all connections are forced to pass through that filter. In a blockchain, the connections are free. Each node can connect to another node without having to go through a higher centralizing element. At least in the public. Private companies can establish their own hierarchy.

In addition to these binary connections, where two nodes connect freely, there is a network formed by the whole set of connections that are made through the protocol that uses the blockchain. Through the use of complex cryptography algorithms, this network allows anyone to manipulate it, it is in charge of validating the transactions verifying that they follow the established characteristics of the chain itself.

One of the key elements in understanding the anonymity and security of the blockchain is undoubtedly cryptography. Using an encryption key, the blockchain converts all the information received into an incomprehensible language for anyone who does not know the encryption key. That is, in the process of transporting information from one node to another, the encrypted information is unusable for any third party who wants to access it. In this way, security reaches extreme levels and ensures the confidentiality of the two users who, after the encryption and decryption process, are the only two capable of using the information in its original and legible form.

Imagine that you write a message on paper in an invented language that only you and your recipient know. If someone took that role, they would be unable to know what it says, because it is written in a language that only you and the person to whom you sent it know. No one else could understand the information you are exchanging. That is what cryptography does. Transforms the information into incomprehensible content and only returns it to its original state once it reaches its goal.

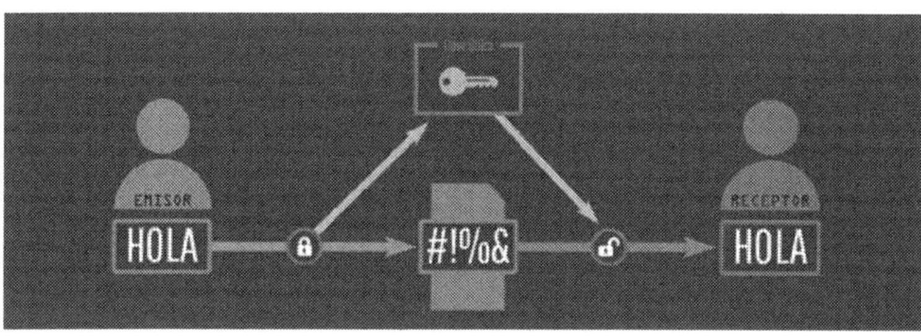

Illustration of NIC.ar that shows the cryptographic process in which a message is only understandable by the sender and the receiver and transformed throughout the process of sending information

Cryptography

An associated and essential concept for the operation of Blockchain technology is cryptography, which gives privacy and security to transactions. There is no use a tool capable of managing a huge amount of information if you are not able to protect it. Who would want to leave their data in an easily accessible place where anyone could take it? Blockchain needs to build trust so that users want to operate on it and deposit their information in the chain, which is what it feeds on. And that gets it through cryptography.

As we have seen before, the operation of cryptography is simple. It converts the information of the sender by means of encryption into illegible and unusable data and decrypts them only when it reaches its receiver, so that during the journey it is nothing more than information transformed into things without apparent meaning and that are not useful for anyone who It was done with her.

There are currently three different types of encryption:

· *Hashing*

Hashing is a type of encryption that always uses the same function to transform information, so that encrypted data always maintains the same form. Imagine that you break a brick with a hammer, every time you did the fragments generated would be different. Now imagine that you cut it with an electric saw always along its longitudinal axis, the result would always be two identical pieces. The latter is what hashing does. Encrypt the information but always using the same pattern, so that a data will always correspond to your hash. This allows, once the information is returned to its original form, to validate that it is correct. If the hash did not match the expected transformation, it is that the information has undergone some kind of manipulation. This is useful in the field of cryptocurrencies, where miners validate the correctness of the data so that they are not manipulated preventing the generation of false virtual money.

Functions are the key to this type of encryption, since they are the way in which information is transformed. These are increasingly sophisticated, and evolve in response to the complexity of the attacks and the good work of cryptanalysts who perform attack tests so that the encryption is prepared before facing real attacks. The obsolete SHA-1 or MD5, which were once glorious, now present vulnerabilities due to the formation of the attackers, and have been replaced by other types of hashes such as SHA-256 and RIPEMD-160, which are what use bitcoin.

There is also the possibility of performing a double hash, that is, that the function re-encrypt an already encrypted data, in a double transformation that provides a more security layer. The ID that identifies each bitcoin transaction is the result of a double hash of type SHA-256.

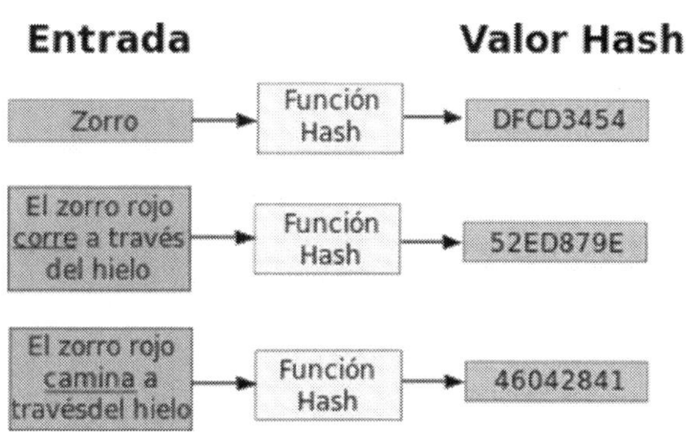

The hashing transforms the incoming information into a numeric key through a function that performs the change, so that the same information always matches the same hash

· *Symmetric cryptography*

This type of cryptography transforms the information by using a code that only the user knows and that acts on the encryption algorithm. This code can be a password or password. The former are random and longer sequences that generate greater security, while the latter are shorter and easier to memorize, since the user usually requires it on numerous occasions in the process of information exchange.

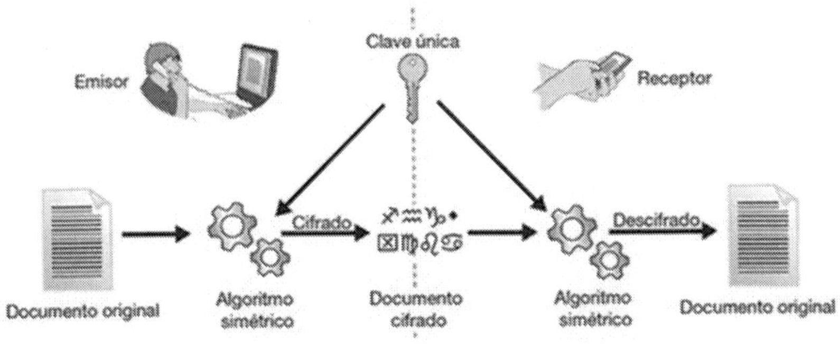

Como muestra el esquema de Minubeinformatica.com, en la criptografía simétrica, a partir de una clave única que actúa sobre el algoritmo de cifrado, la información original se encripta y desencripta al inicio y al final de la transmisión.

One of the most used algorithms that work through the use of symmetric keys is the Advanced Encryption Standard (AES), which generates keys of more than seventy digits. It is the one used by Bitcoin. A larger code size, greater security, but also more computing power is necessary to decipher and work with them, and that is why one of the challenges of the networks that use cryptocurrencies is their high energy use.

· *Asymmetric cryptography*

This type of encryption combines the use of two keys, one public and one private, which are somehow linked to complete the encryption process. The private one must be kept secret and should only be known by the owner of the information, while the public one is used to manage and share this information with other users.

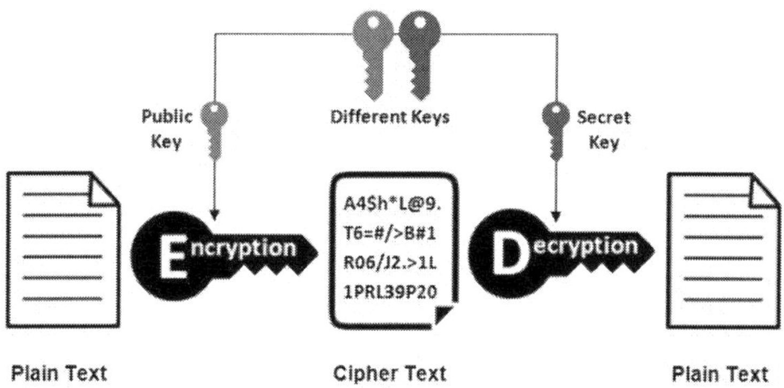

Medium scheme that shows how in asymmetric cryptography two keys are necessary: a public one that encrypts the information and a secret one that decrypts it

The private key acts on the public so that it can complete the encryption and decryption process, but it does not happen the other way around. That is, knowing only the public key one cannot access all the information in which it is involved.

In the use of bitcoins, private keys are random numbers in the hexadecimal system that combine numbers from 0 to 9 in pairs and letters from A to F. Only these are able to move the bitcoins associated with them, so it is essential own them Even if a ụser has bitcoins deposited in a currency exchange or a purse, he must ensure that he also has control of the private keys, as it is the only thing he can use to recover them in case of platform closure or attempted theft.

Current technology does not allow to find out a private key from a public key, so revealing the latter to operate does not pose any danger. The encryption operation of Bitcoin technology is as follows: from the issuer's private key, a public key is generated by elliptic curve cryptography (ECDSA). During the transaction to this key a SHA256 hash encryption is applied, then a transformation is applied that hides the hash obtained and also decreases the size, and then it is encoded in the BASE58 algorithm to make it more readable. This triple filtering generates the address that allows the recipient to receive transactions.

The private key is the only one capable of changing the authorship of cryptocurrencies, so all cyber-attacks that claim to steal them should be directed to that key. Today, that is impossible, since the elliptic curve cryptography should be reversed.

Practical exercise 5

Set what type of encryption each scheme represents:

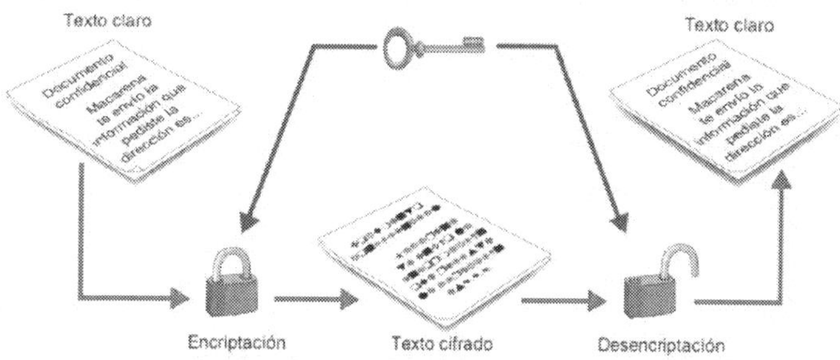

Hashing	Symmetric cryptography	Asymmetric cryptography

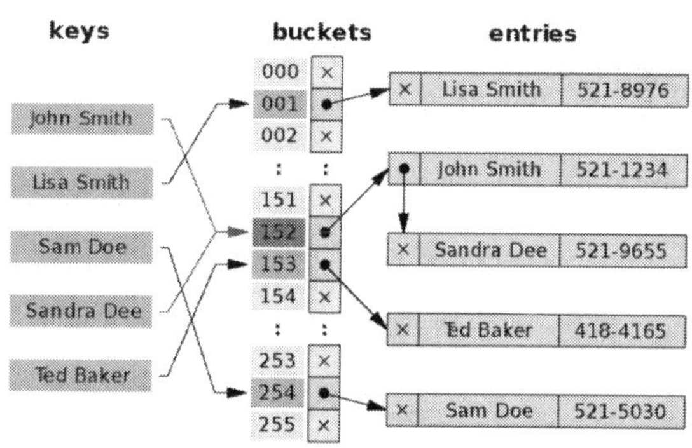

Hashing	Symmetric cryptography	Asymmetric cryptography

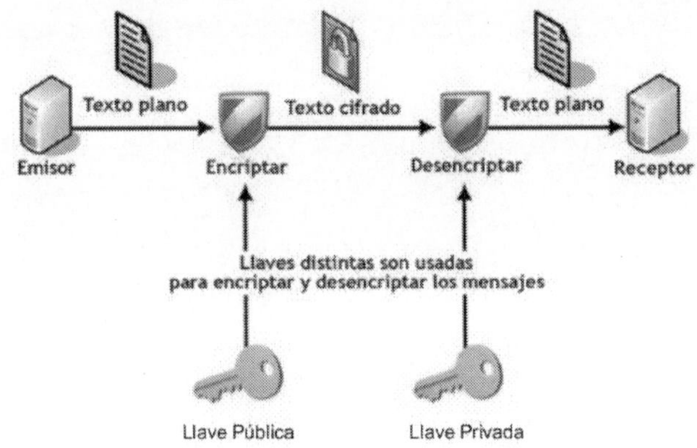

Hashing	Symmetric cryptography	Asymmetric cryptography

The blocks of the chain

What is really a block of the blockchain? It is nothing more than a set of transactions that are stored in the chain. It would be a file cabinet inside the large bookcase that is the chain. This filing cabinet contains the information of various transactions, and once complete it is placed in order next to the rest of the filing cabinets or blocks. All copies of blockchains keep those filers in the same order, so that all the files contained maintain a revisable logic.

The first part of each block is called a header. It contains the hash of the previous block, so that it can stand behind it and maintain order. It is an encrypted data that allows the blocks to be sorted one after the other in succession. In the header is also the difficulty, a parameter that miners have to solve to validate the block. Miners, using computer equipment, test random numbers until they find the difficulty parameter. It's as if we were trying to open a safe by trying random combinations. This parameter is complicated or facilitated so that the time to solve each block is 10 minutes. The nonce, which is also in the header, is a 32-bit number that can only be used once and prevents a block, once validated, from being manipulated again.

Beyond the header, the block has all the information that is stored in it and also a hash, which is the result of the encryption of its content. Each block has a unique hash, so if its content is altered, the hash would change, and the chain in which such an alteration is made would not be validated and therefore voided.

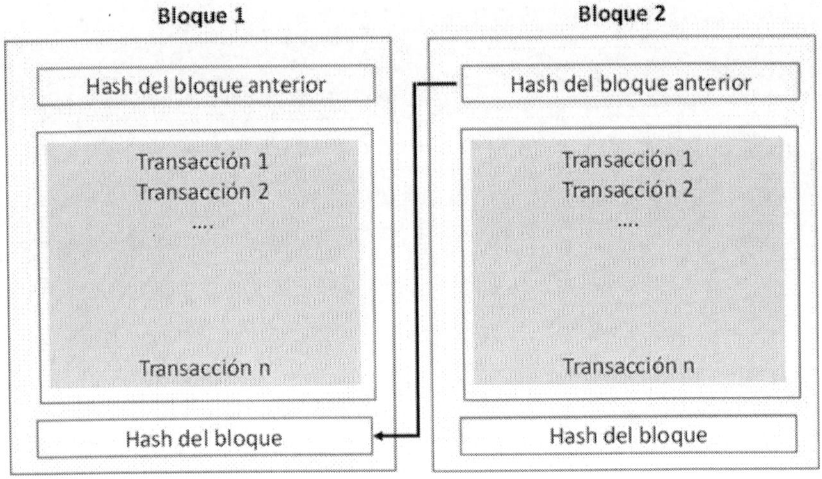

Diagram of a block according to Loyolaandnews.es that shows the correlation through the hashes of the header that allow its ordering in the chain

Ejercicio práctico 6

The difficulty of a block is a parameter that is adjusted so that the mining time of each block remains constant regardless of the number of miners that are working. Therefore, choose the correct option in each statement:

· If the number of miners decreases, the difficulty parameter… UP / DOWN

· If the number of miners increases, the difficulty parameter… UP / DOWN

· If the number of miners is maintained, but these increase the mining power, the difficulty parameter… UP / DOWN

Proof of work (PoW)

Remember that a blockchain works in the same way for all its users since the rules of its use are included in its programming and each transaction is validated by the chain members.

Imagine that some of the users do not agree with its operation or would like to act against it for your benefit. Let's say, for example, that a Bitcoin user would like to change the blockchain to redirect several transactions outside their own wallet and get rich. It would be necessary for there to be some method that annulled the malicious actions of these traitors to the chain's consensus, and the most used of these are the work tests, a procedure that validates the transactions to ensure that they comply with the rules established in the chain .

Proofs of Work (PoW) is the method that Bitcoin uses to secure consensus, but there are other methods used by other types of chains. In this system, the nodes compete with each other to perform cryptographic checks. Users of the chain that so wish, called miners, can intervene to make checks so as to ensure that the transactions are correct, valid, and obey the consensus algorithm. To do this, their devices try to solve a complex mathematical calculation through random tests until, by chance, they find the numbering that verifies that the transaction and its encryption match the way the blockchain works. The first miner to verify the transaction, gets a reward in the form of bitcoins, which encourages many users to become these miners.

On a more technical level, the miners act on the blocks that are waiting to be added to the chain, that is, those that contain the information of transactions not yet verified. To verify and add them, they have to find a number less than the limit value established by the difficulty. The first miner who gets it receives bonuses in cryptocurrencies or commissions, provided that the rest also validate the operation. Therefore, validation is not a matter of an independent node, but of many actors in the process.

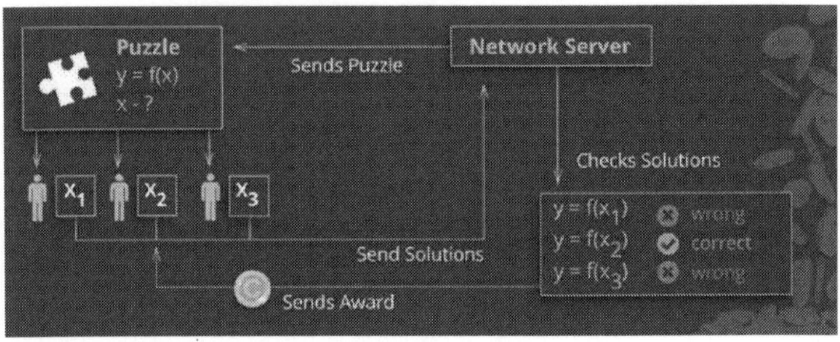

Cointelegraph scheme that shows how miners compete to solve the mathematical calculation that validates the transaction, receiving the reward only the first to do so

The commissions received encourage more users to act as miners. Mining is expensive, requires high energy expenditure. The more the chain grows, the more energy is required. While blocks with home computers could be validated at first, a much greater mining power is now required. Even many miners organize to jointly invest and acquire sufficient mining power. Thus, commissions on bitcoin transactions are necessary to pay these security guards that make the network stay and prevent its manipulation.

It is true that miners also receive benefits in the form of cryptocurrencies, but these bonuses are reduced over time. Every 210,000 mined blocks triggers the halving effect that cuts mining benefits in half. That is, it costs more and more to undermine and is received less in the form of virtual currencies. Therefore, an additional incentive in the form of commissions is necessary. The more difficult the process of verification is, more commissions are necessary.

Practical exercise 7

To see if you have understood how Proofs of Work works as a validation method for the chain, think about the following questions:

A) The maximum amount of bitcoins is limited to 21 million units. When all of them are mined, do you think the mining will be over and therefore the work tests?

B) Do you think bitcoins would be sustainable if there were no commissions on transactions?

C) What could happen if a hardware company develops a new hyperefficient mining system?

Proof of Stake (PoS)

Another way to verify different transactions using other types of Blockchain is the Proofs of Stake. In this case, for the user to become a verifier, he must have a minimum amount of funds in the chain that he must keep without mobilizing. The higher the funds, the higher the chances of being chosen to validate the transaction, and the more benefits you can get. That is, the user who acts as a watchman so that the transaction is correct is chosen at random, but more likely depending on the amount of cryptocurrencies he has in his portfolio. The miners in this case are called validators or verifiers, and the mining process is called coining or forging.

This system eliminates competition for mining power. Simply simply have a good amount of funds held in the portfolio. In principle, it would thus eliminate centralization by mining power, in which those who have the most mining capacity have more relevance in the validation process. If mining costs continue to increase in work tests, fewer and fewer people would have access to the verification process and there would be a risk that a few could have control over the chain. On the other hand, this participation test system is more accessible and allows access to a greater number of users, although it does not fail to favor those who have more reserved funds.

In the case of Proofs of Work, if someone wanted to control the network they would need to have 51% of the total computing power of mining. In the case of participation tests, it is necessary to have 51% of the total cryptocurrency funds. In this case, if someone wanted to buy more virtual currencies to control it, with each purchase the price of this would increase and it would be more and more economically expensive to get new acquisitions, which would make it impossible to reach the necessary 51%.

Despite the energy advantage of participation tests, they have been running for less time and have yet to prove their efficiency and true potential.

The main cryptocurrencies that use this method are Dash, Factom, Nav Coin, Stellar, Neo...

Proof of stake PoS	**Proof of work**
-Ecological, since minimum resources are required for the chain to work.	-A lot of electricity consumption. Today the electricity consumption of a small country is needed to secure the chain of the PoW system.
-Decentralized Participation System.	-Incentive centralized mining farms.
-Little knowledge is required to run PoS nodes.	-It is necessary to have technical knowledge to optimize GPU (ETH) and ASIC (BTC) graphics cards.
-Once started, it doesn't stop.	-It requires constant technical adjustments to reduce costs.
-Rewards for transactions remains in the one that generates the block.	-Transaction rewards goes to miners.

Medium chart that classifies the different tests

Practical exercise 8

In this case, we will also reflect, but on the Proofs of Stake:

A) Do you think the Proof of Stake method favors or harms new cryptocurrencies?

B) Do you consider it more equitable since the possibility of receiving rewards no longer depends on the power of mining?

What would happen if associations emerged that grouped capital to have an advantage in the Proof of Stake?

Open Source

In most cases, Blockchain technology uses open source. This means that any user can access its programming and view its content and operation. Recall that in the blockchain itself the consensus rules are inscribed, the rules of the game accepted by all who operate on it and that make everyone participate in the same conditions. Open source allows you to verify at any time that they remain intact.

In turn, the fact that everyone can access the code that determines the operation of the chain, makes any expert can suggest improvements, so that the software can have a multitude of selfless workers who provide valuable suggestions that make the chain improve again and again. If there is a vulnerability, a legion of followers is available to find the solution.

There are many types of software that choose to use open source to improve and develop such as Linux, Firefox, Android, WordPress...

The Bitcoin protocol, of course, is public and open source. Bitcoin does not have an owner, so in the end its own users manage it. Since all of them must use the same version to interact, it is this need for homogenization that causes the new variations to be integrated or not depending on the acceptance of developers, users, miners and all those who operate on the chain of blocks. It is this acceptance that regulates possible dissensions or bifurcations. Specifically, the license used by Bitcoin is called the MIT License.

Public blockchains have open source, but this does not mean that private blockchains do not. The latter can choose between open or closed code. Keeping the code open, even among a small and limited number of people, reflects transparency. Or what is the same, that although there are very few participants, they play with the cards in sight and without traps.

In closed-source blockchains where control over it is of a limited number of people, it is more difficult to verify that the established norms remain unchanged. In this case, trust lies in the word of its owners, which implies a setback in the generation of consensus and trust. If the rules can be inscribed in the chain itself and in the sight of everyone, why hide them?

There is also a middle ground between open source and closed code. Many blockchains are advertised as open, but they may have some hidden code. You have to be very careful with this guy. However, being partially or totally private does not necessarily mean that you have something to hide, but simply wants to protect part of your development so that it is not copied. If it can be replicated, it is more difficult to maintain exclusivity and monetization could be more complicated. They may simply be trying to protect the technology they intend to sell.

Practical exercise 9

Cross out those statements that you think do not match an open source software:

1) Access to your source code is free and can be modified by anyone

2) Software improvements are limited and restricted

3) Any user can use it freely

4) It can be used freely, but always after having asked permission from its creator; otherwise, it would be a crime

5) It has no updates

6) It usually has many viruses

7) It usually has large communities around it

8) They are usually quite cheap and cheap products

Their protocols are usually more flexible and their compatibility problems are less.

Blockchain authentication

One of the most interesting aspects of blockchains is their safety. This does not arise as an added benefit, but as a necessity. If the objective of Blockchain is to manage and manage millions and millions of data, it would not make sense that they would not travel safely and could be accessible to anyone. Why are you going to build the best transportation system in the world if you can steal your merchandise on each trip?

Confidentiality is one of the important aspects in the Blockchain security environment. In the process of transmitting the information, only the sender and the receiver have access to it due to the encryption process. But if the chain is also private, the security is even greater. Any stranger would need to first have access to the chain itself, and then to the information that several of its members are exchanged.

Therefore, only users interested in the exchange have access to the information. But what if these users were not what they claim to be? It is necessary that the authentication process that connects the user with the chain be effective. These validation processes are more intense in the private chains, since in the public the exchange is more sporadic and only requires authentication at the time of the transaction.

As it is not necessary to provide personal data in public chains to participate, it is important that the chain has a security system that ensures the transaction, that is, that the issuer cannot avoid the agreed transaction or the recipient reject it by abusing its anonymity . This is solved by the chain's own operation. If the exchange is agreed, all copies of the chain execute it, and at the moment in which one of the two interested parties punctually alters it, that manipulation would be rejected by contrasting with the rest of the copies of the chain that already They have validated.

That is, it could not back down because the rest of the nodes act as witnesses to their decision.

Another key factor in the security of Blockchain when it comes to building trust between sender and receiver is the ability to keep the information unchanged, which cannot be changed either voluntarily or involuntarily. In this sense, since each transaction has to be validated by the rest of the chain users, it is practically impossible that it can be modified at a specific point. The rest of the unaltered chain would serve as a mold and mirror to verify that this modification does not correspond to the rest of the copies, and would automatically cancel the transaction if this is not the expected one.

Given this scenario, what would happen if all copies of the chain were changed in the same way and at the same time? It would be necessary that 51% of the copies validate the false transaction, that is, that more than half of the copies of the existing blockchains perform the same manipulation. In the case of Bitcoin or public chains, it is practically impossible that by having so many users, most of them agreed to cause such alteration. In private companies, the lower the number of users, the greater the likelihood of an alteration agreement. Although, after all, it would be a new consensus of the majority.

The Blockhain Balance

Several of the characteristics of the blockchain affect each other, so they have to be taken into account when designing them, enhancing those that interest you most. Specifically, the most significant are its security, its scalability and its decentralization.

The Bitcoin and Ethereum chains try to strengthen their decentralization and security, so their weak point is scalability. As the chains grow, more computing power and electrical spending are necessary for them to work, and transactions become slower. Let's not forget that these must be verified by the users, and the more they are done and the more users exist, the complexity of the process increases significantly.

The solution would be that only a few nodes in the chain could validate the transactions to avoid more complex interactions and give simplicity to the process, but in that case, decentralization would be irretrievably lost. These nodes would have more power, they would be more important than the rest. Security would also be lost. Each user would no longer be a verification center, so that a manipulation or error could prosper, it would only have to circumvent the few selected verification nodes.

Thus, depending on the objective of each blockchain, you will have to assess which characteristics to enhance and which to sacrifice. If freedom and equality are sought, decentralization cannot be compromised. If speed is sought in the process to match other systems, decentralization must be sacrificed.

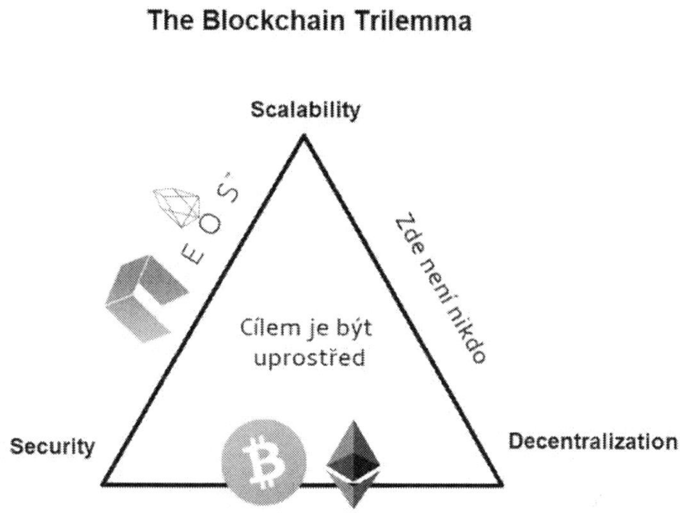

The blockchain trilemma, as Kryptomagazin shows, is the need to sacrifice some characteristics to enhance others between scalability, security and decentralization. Applications like Bitcoin or Ethereum opt for security and decentralization, while others like Neo sacrifice decentralization to gain scalability

Practical exercise 10

Choose which two characteristics you would enhance and which one you would sacrifice in the blockchain developed for the following projects:

A) Juan wants to develop an application through which two users from any part of the world can exchange their homes for a set time. It would serve, for example, so that two families could change their homes for a month to go on vacation to another country for free, only by lending the houses.

B) María wants to develop a company in which users from all over the world can freely exchange objects of her choice and uses blockchain to avoid fraud, but wants to charge commission for each transaction.

Roberto wants to make an app in his company in which anonymously, each worker can express their complaints and exchange them with the members they deem appropriate.

Types of blockchains

Different block chains can be as many as these are designed for a certain function. Depending on the practical application for which it was created, some of its characteristics are enhanced or given more importance. However, these tend to be classified into two large groups, public and private, and derived from both.

Public blockchains

Any user can access them. There is no restriction that prevents seeing the activity stored in them and anyone can use them, therefore its transparency is maximum. Any manipulation could be easily reached by anyone with the right knowledge. There are no administrators and anonymity is absolute. Its database is distributed in bulk and can be maintained by users who wish, and in fact participate in its development and maintenance through proofs of work or Stake is usually rewarded.

Private blockchains

Prior permission is required to interact with them, so despite sharing technology, many users do not consider them pure block chains. The databases are on specific servers not open to the public. That is why they are centralized, users require the approval of their owners, who have access to all the information, and also have the necessary control to modify the blockchain.

By limiting the number of users and these are generally reduced, the cost is minimal and the problems of scalability of public blockchains do not appear. In addition, it is not necessary for all participants to validate the transactions; a few nodes designated for this would suffice.

Regarding privacy, they have the advantage that no one who has not been granted permission to access can intervene in the information managed.

Hybrid

They are not usually open to the public and are controlled by entities, although they do use an open source, which can be freely observed and consulted. That is, their use is limited under a permit but they do show openly the way they work. It is usually used by governments.

Consortium Networks

It is a private network that acts on a part of a blockchain that is public that accepts the integration of certain nodes of the first. It is necessary to obtain permission to act on them but the fact of operating through open systems generates a certain degree of trust since it makes use of public protocols.

Practical exercise 11

It establishes to which type of network each of the following characteristics belongs, public (PU), private (PR) or federated / consortium (FC):

	PU	PR	FC
Anyone can access			
Previous permission is required necesita			
ID is required			
Participation is anonymous			
Decentralized algorithms			
Own algorithms			
Slow transaction speed			
Fast transaction speed			

WHAT IS BLOCKCHAIN USED FOR?

The revolutionary capacity for security, data management and trust generation of blockchains makes it attractive for all those activities or companies that require databases. The features provided by this new system are so beneficial that compared to the rest, they generate the feeling that whoever does not use Blockchain is doomed to other more archaic and insecure alternatives. That is why there are more and more entities and organizations that incorporate them into their management, giving them a great diversity of applications. Although Bitcoin was its first use in 2009, the appearance of Ethereum in 2014 and its smart contracts allowed us to see beyond cryptocurrencies in terms of the blockchain and between 2015 and 2016 an explosion of startups that use Blockchain for their applications was generated . Today, new uses are constantly coming out and hopefully in the future blockchains will be integrated into almost every aspect of our lives.

Blockhain on the bench

In addition to its usefulness for the birth of Bitcoin, blockchains have also been used by those entities that were significantly threatened by their launch: banking entities. In order to compete with the security of bitcoin, financial institutions have had no choice but to incorporate Blockchain technology so as not to fall behind in benefits.

Over time, banking has always depended on the trust it has been able to show to its customers. Their representatives have always struggled to show the strength of their entity and, face to face, they try to create a relationship of mutual trust to retain their users. However, a personal-based relationship always leaves a loophole to distrust. On the other hand, the programmed security of Blockchain is unperturbed, maximum, and against that it is impossible to compete.

This means that in countries where banks have a worse perception on the part of society, Blockchain becomes an effective alternative. In countries like Mexico or Cyprus, where trust in banking is deteriorated, the new economic system offered by the blockchain has greater acceptance in society, which causes more and more users to join the unbanked population. Also in countries where inflation or currency is unstable there is a great leap to crypto economics.

Another aspect in which the bank is forced to use Blockchain if it does not want to end up replaced by it is in the interconnectivity. While the different branches of the same entity may have different regulations and protocols depending on the country in which they operate, the blockchain is not governed by a particular legislation due to its ubiquity status. This allows Blockchain-based banks to unify their protocols according to the unified characteristics of the blockchain on which they operate and share.

What is clear is that the first use of Blockchain was to create an alternative to the established banking system, and that this threatened bank must make use of this technology if it wants to survive it in a kind of whiting that bites its tail.

This is the case of Ripple, a platform for interbank international payments that aims to unify transactions and make them safer and faster. It is an open system in which anyone can participate in principle, but its users must be previously accepted by the system, which makes its operation more like a private blockchain than a public one. Other platforms through which banking takes advantage of Blockchain are R3 or Hyperledger, and surely they are only a small example of the large number of alternatives that will be created in the future.

Another financial aspect to consider in which Blockchain has much to say is in the granting of loans. To receive a bank loan, today we depend on prior approval, on an initial study of our possibilities, and the bank finally decides whether to grant the loan or not. The blockchain could eliminate this arbitrary intermediary at a stroke through smart contracts between users. These contracts establish the conditions of the transactions between the person who makes the loan and the one who receives it. It could also lead to auctions in which the lenders competed to lend their money in a free fight, always with the clear and agreed conditions through the exchange contract.

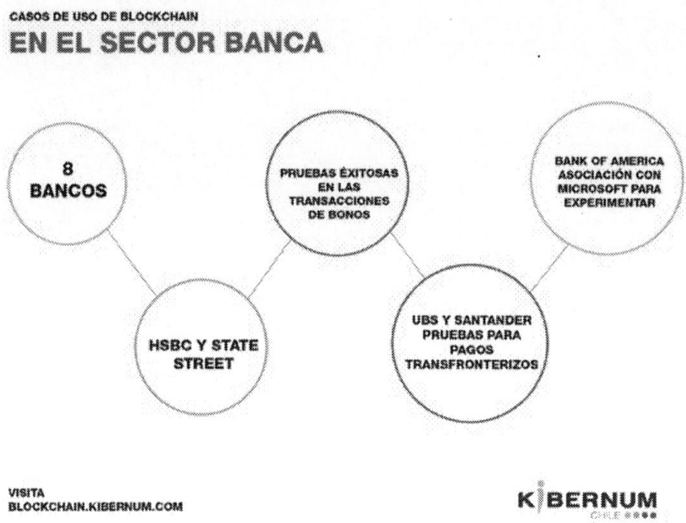

Kibernum illustration that shows how banking implements blockchain technology not to be left behind technologically

Practical exercise 12

The bank has had to make use of the strategy "if you can't the enemy join him" to survive Blockchain technology. In this regard, reflect:

A) What elements do you think powers and sacrifices banking in the Blockchain trilemma?

B) Banking may survive Blockchain technology using its digital features, but do you think it will be able to counteract its power of decentralization in the future?

Internet of things

The so-called "internet of things" tries to organize as much information as possible and analyze it as a person would do to save the work of consulting the information, studying it, selecting it and finally taking advantage of it.

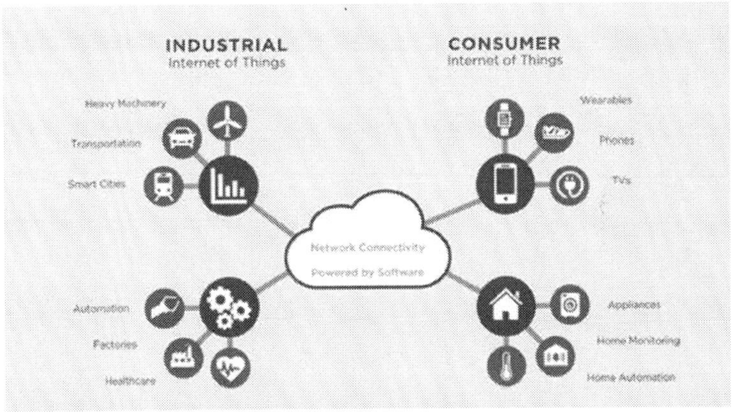

As this illustration of i-SCOOP shows, the "internet of things" tries to relate all the information possible so that both companies and consumers can get the most optimal form of what they need for their life or business function

This objective makes no sense in the current centralized services, which use this information process for their own benefit. This idea would exponentially increase their chances if anyone could contribute their grain of sand, if it were intervention and free consultation.

In the current situation, its progress is limited to the centralizing nuclei that, in addition, could include their own bias without ensuring that the information must always be true. If these databases are used as queries and have a centralizing element, it will give priority to that information that is most profitable.

Imagine that a server tries to process all the information related to different television models, accumulating all existing models, characteristics of each, user experiences, sales data of the different models ... If a person would like to use this database to Knowing which TV is more suitable for her, this centralized platform could give more importance to data related to a particular brand that could sponsor it. That could not happen with Blockchain technology, where all users could freely provide their information, without giving priority to one over another, and it would be the algorithm of the chain, undisturbed and decided among its users, that would analyze it in the pre-established way. In that sense, IBM and Filament are developing decentralized alternatives.

Practical exercise 13

In this exercise we will reflect on the need for the decentralization of the "internet of things". Imagine that you are the owner of a platform responsible for collecting and managing sports equipment so that, a user looking for the best shoe for him, by introducing a series of parameters such as frequency of use, budget, preferred material, sole size and others, The platform offers you a specific shoe.

If a shoe brand proposed an economic agreement for you to show your brand instead of others even if they are more suited to the search parameters, would it be fair? Could you do it by using Blockchain?

Bilateral agreements through smart contracts

Smart Contracts are more a tool than an application, but due to the infinite number of possible uses it is a use to take into account. Smart contracts are conditions that two people establish for an exchange and that are established in the blockchain forcing compliance.

Any agreement is sealed with this type of contract. Imagine that a company sells virtual courses at a rate of € 200 per module, and that these come out monthly. Once the contract was signed, the company would automatically send the module every month and in turn also receive the amount stipulated automatically. Smart contracts generate absolute trust that, being decentralized, cannot be violated by either party.

No users can break the pact because the content would already be ready to be sent and payments scheduled and prepared at the time of signing the contract.

Decentralization and encryption of blockchains are adequate to seal agreements between two people without the intervention of outsiders. For this, the conditions of the transaction are established in the chain itself and it is this automatically that executes the exchange under the terms established in it.

These terms are sealed in the so-called Smart contracts or smart contracts, which establish the characteristics of the exchange. Once accepted by the two interested parties, the blockchain acts in accordance with the consensual orders of the participants, forcing them to accept the agreed conditions and acting as an immovable manager of the transaction.

This person-to-person relationship eliminates intermediaries, thus accelerating the process and eliminating bureaucratic and specialized personnel expenses. The applications of such contracts are endless; there are as many options as agreements can be made between people.

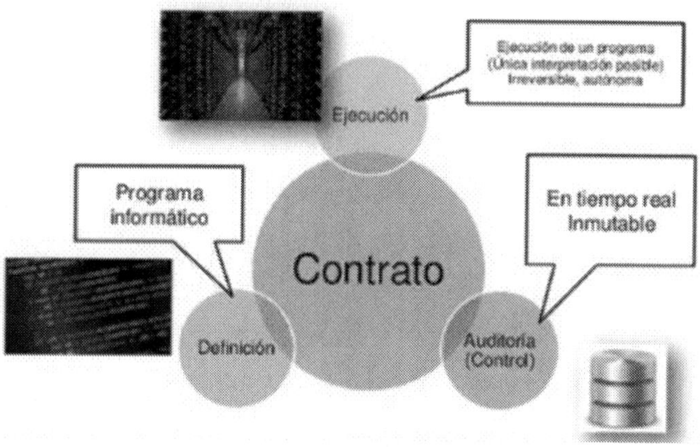

As this Criptonetwork scheme shows, a smart contract is a program defined by the characteristics of the agreement, validated by the blockchain so that it cannot be modified, and that is executed irreversibly and automatically when the conditions established for it are met.

Practical exercise 14

It establishes the conditions in a contract for the sale of a home that will be paid in installments. It includes the necessary triggers, what actions would trigger consequences and what these would be. Remember that the whole process must be automated.

Insurance security

Another sector that can benefit from the implementation of Blockchain is that of insurance companies. In recent years, insurance companies have seen how comparator platforms have become the main customer selectors.

These platforms include the information of the different brands and are shown to the potential customer, as a catalog, so that you can select the best option. Moreover, many of these platforms dare to decide for themselves which one is best for the client, so that this saves the cumbersome work of seeking information, contrasting it, and even deciding.

This makes insurance companies forced to compete. To know the scales that handle these platforms and to try to position themselves as best as possible in them. If they are excluded, they remain out of the pie distribution.

In this sense, in an environment in which the collection and organization of information becomes vital, future (and not so future) advances in data management such as the internet of things, Big Data or cognitive intelligence , find a fundamental rolc. And of course, in this process of data management, also blockchain.

At a stroke, the client could access hundreds of data from the different insurance companies in a safe and anonymous way, and in the opposite direction, the companies themselves also benefit from the management of technical, expert, internal and external communication data. ... The process would be automated advantageously for all members of the process.

Another way to fight against the increasingly high competition in the insurance sector is to join with each other to combat these attrition struggles between them, and an example of this is the creation of consortia such as that established by Aegon, Allianz, Munich, Zurich and Swiss. Through Blockchain Insurance Industry Intiative they use blockchain technology to share useful information for each other under the characteristics of this blockchain previously agreed upon by them.

B3i is a consortium of insurers that use Blockchain to improve their services, as CriptoNoticias shows

Similarly, smart contracts could also expedite the work of insurers, so that, once a service has been contracted, if it is subject to objective conditions, the relevant remuneration is established automatically.

Imagine that we buy a car whose insurance gives us that in the event of any engine failure in the first three years of use, it is automatically changed to a new one. In the event of such a failure, the client could activate his benefit without the intervention of a third party, or of an expert or the insurer itself, since this would be established in the bases of the blockchain.

This would expedite the work of the insurer and in turn increase the client's confidence by eliminating human barriers. He would not have to answer or plead with anyone since the terms of the contract would be activated immediately.

Another practical example would be the insurance for agriculture. In the case of hailstorms, floods or droughts that end up with some kind of crop, the weather data of the nearby stations could be sufficient to activate the remuneration of all those insurances that were affected by these conditions without the intervention of third parties.

Practical exercise 15

Become for a few moments in a commercial of a company that implements blockchain technology in other businesses. List three advantages with which you could convince an insurance company to access it:

-

-

Military uses

Most technological inventions find their first application in the military environment and Blockchain also has much to contribute in that regard.

As a secure information transfer system, blockchain provides a more secure environment with its encryption, acting as a shielded messaging system. Communications in the military field are everything, and where historically always undecipherable codes have been sought, Blockchain can appear as the definitive solution.

Also in the management of the database can be useful in the gigantic task of organizing military equipment, human resources, exchanges between the different bases, not to mention the ability to allow or block the use of weapons or military vehicles as required by the situation.

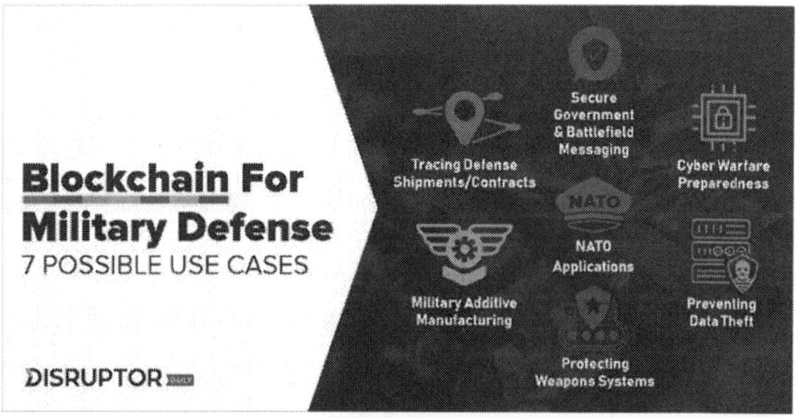

Illustration of Daily Disruptor that shows possible military uses of Blockchain: communications security, traceability of movement and manufacturing of materials, cyber warfare, military applications, data security...

Practical exercise 16

During World War II, the United States Army used the Navajo language to encode all messages during the Pacific War.

A) What type of encryption does this strategy remind you of?

Making a simile with this strategy and through the already known advantages of the blockchain, it lists several advantages that the use of Blockchain in military communications could provide.

Copyright

In the case of the preservation of copyright, it would be possible to include in the blockchain the information of the authorship of a certain artistic work. Since the blockchain organizes the information chronologically, one block after another, it would be possible to establish who was the first to register its authorship, establishing itself as the real author.

Authorship without centralized platforms dedicated to it would be demonstrated. The author could also benefit financially from his works through smart contracts that establish that each download or use will activate a transaction of a certain cost for his wallet.

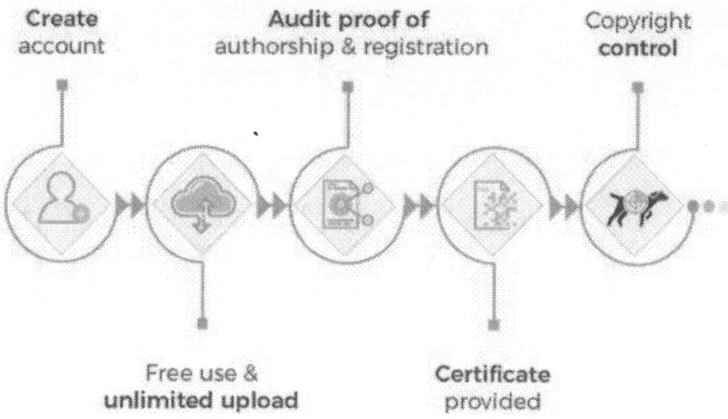

Coinoks scheme showing copyright management through the use of the chain. A work would be free to use until it is registered and approved in the chain, which would serve as evidence to validate and prove authorship

Practical exercise 17

Spotify is a popular music content playback application that pays authors who share their content based on the views they receive. What would be the main advantage of establishing a similar system through Blockchain?

Blockchain in telecommunications

The unifying power of Blockchain as a core in data and information management can be clearly seen in the telecommunications industry. Each brand has its own database, its infrastructure, its communication system, its logistics, which together between the different companies results in a competitive chaos for the information that does not generate anything other than a brutal economic attrition for each of the parts that could be softened by a unified structure: and that is what the blockchain provides.

Unification through Blockchain would also avoid the need to make some systems compatible with others. In order for a user of a certain telemarketer to be able to contact another of a different brand, it is necessary that both protocols be granted specific permissions to be able to access and exchange information, something that would be solved with the use of a common blockchain so that All users will use the same communication protocol and access to the database.

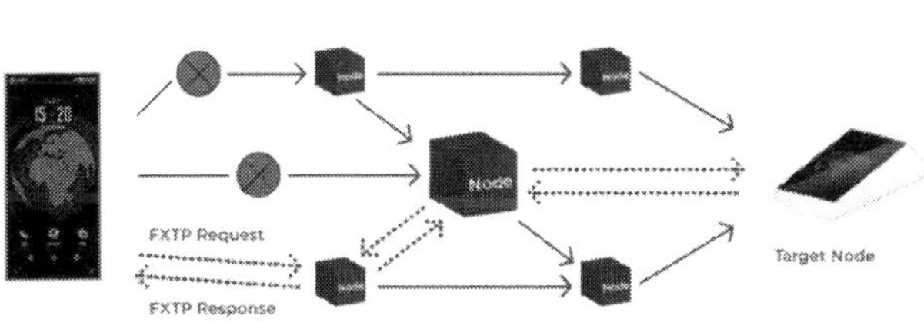

Blockchain can act as a network in which two devices can connect through their nodes anywhere in the world, as bitcobie shows

In terms of security, the telecommunications sector also benefits from the blockchain. Blockchain is invulnerable to external aspects, which, taking into account the amount of sensitive information we share through the internet and telephony, would no longer be an advance, but a need not to compromise user information.

Similarly, in relation to the SIM cards of the phones, they have to go through successive and tedious control protocols to protect their security. They are monitored when they are created, when they are sent to the points of sale, when they are delivered to their customers, when they are finally activated ... Acting directly on the blockchain and with the security conditions that it allows, it would alleviate both process and download so many verifications, granting more security in the global process by offering fewer points of vulnerability.

And what about customer control over their own data? Have you ever wondered where tele-operators get your contact information to call you incessantly and offer you their services? Well, the implementation of Blockchain would allow greater control of their personal data to customers, granting permissions in an encrypted manner and granting their credentials only at the really necessary points and, under a smart contract, so that they are only usable in certain actions . The tedious commercials that use our data at discretion for unwanted tasks are over.

Practical exercise 18

Imagine that a new company wants to enter the telecommunications universe. What initial difficulties would you encounter with respect to other companies? How could Blockchain solve it? Would this be useful for consumers?

Voting and democracy

What better than to count votes in an immovable and non-manipulable registration system to ensure the transparency of a vote? The blockchain, being a historical record that places one transaction after another, could act as a perfect counting system.

Since the information is encrypted, the vote would be secret, and by giving each person a unique identifier, they would only be allowed to vote once, in the same way that the same bitcoin cannot be used twice. And all users could act as validators of transactions, that is, of votes.

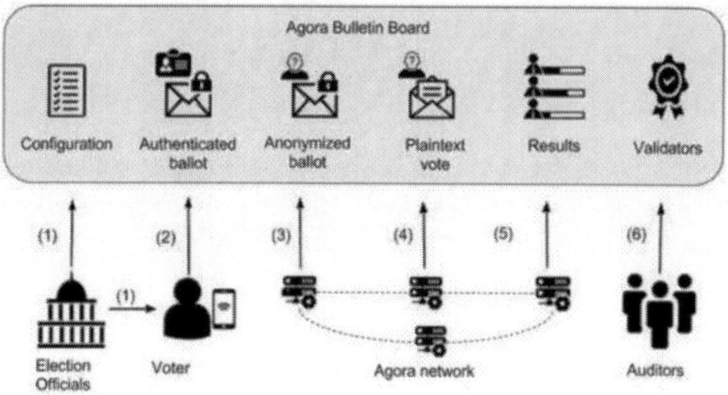

This RFI scheme shows how each voter with their unique ID becomes an anonymous voter through encryption and their voting information is used (and validated by the rest of the chain members) to generate the results

Practical exercise 19

Reflect on how Blockchain could improve citizen participation and therefore democracy in advanced countries.

Independent energy

The energy sector, so "far" from customer understanding, with incomprehensible bills, can also be reconverted with the emergence of Blockchain technology.

Currently, energy sources are small and isolated. A single power plant can supply a large region, so that the energy communication system resembles the current operation of the Internet, where information is exchanged between small concrete networks with large central servers.

But the energy future will be different. The different energy sources will vary, they will be distributed geographically in a different way and they will distribute the energy with more options than now. Even many people already establish their own consumption with solar panels. This means that the energy nuclei are going to become wider networks, with more access points, all interconnected with each other and not so dependent on a centralizing factor. That is to say: the use and distribution of energy will be decentralized. And as energy does, so will all the necessary information for that process, making more independent technological systems necessary and capable of encompassing wider networks.

Currently, the distribution of energy depends on government mediation, but in view is the failure of governments that allow higher and higher bills and suspicious and corrupt contracts of politicians with energy entities. This will mean that in the not too distant future people will seek energy independence, and for this, smart contracts will be necessary to establish the conditions that they are willing to support, and not those imposed by agreements between government and business that are unfavorable. .

Without going any further, Siemens has already made use of Blockchain technology through the LO3 company which, in agreement with ConsenSys, already experiences a decentralized energy distribution system in Brooklyn. There, a community network has been developed in which energy is generated, stored and distributed locally.

As for the future of self-consumption, many families choose to get their own energy with photovoltaic panels. While in some times of the year they produce more energy than they use, in others the opposite occurs. This means that in some times they have an energy surplus and in others a deficiency, which could generate a self-consumption energy exchange market. Here Blockchain smart contracts would become a vital tool for the sale of self-consumption energy. Powerpeers, in Holland, already allows the exchange of energy between two points thanks to the blockchain.

A smart contract includes the conditions of sale of energy from a house with surplus of its own production to another that needs it

Practical exercise 20

Currently governments, to maintain the energy lobby, hinder the generation of home energy. In 2015 they approved the sun tax (although currently repealed), and the transfer of energy that is not through commercialization companies is penalized. Do you think that Blockchain can be used to avoid government obstacles in the free distribution of energy?

More security in the field of security

However peliculero sounds the use of identification cards to enter the different sections of government buildings or reputable companies, Blockchain will make current uses obsolete with the contributions that can be granted to access systems.

Let's say you have a company where you only want certain people to have access to higher levels. At present, the cards act as a key that only allow the holder to enter, which is still an extension of the classic and rudimentary system of the physical key. The possible card accesses are programmed on the carrier card, which respond to a central database. And there is the problem.

Anyone who manipulates the company's software could modify the data on their card and get the desired access. It would be enough to know programming or have a good contact to bribe. In the end, everything would depend on the human factor, since there is that possibility of modification.

However, Blockchain would prevent it de facto. Recall that the chain is not a program in itself that can be modified, it would require that all copies of the chain be changed; that is, that all those teams that act as a node, agreed to perform corruption.

The permits would act automatically and without the possibility of being changed in an interested and individualized way. What is programmed in the chain becomes unbreakable norms.

Practical Exercise 21

In addition to access control through Blockchain-based cards, can you think of any other advantage that the blockchain could have in terms of security practice?

The Fourth Industrial Revolution

Mass commerce begins to be affected by custom manufacturing. While so far the factories were based on making thousands of equal products to be sold right and left, the truth is that more and more success is in differentiation and personalization.

The common is no longer attractive. No one wants to have what others have. The consumer seeks exclusivity, to tell Apple. Selling what is accessible to the vast majority is rather a commercial setback. And that is why industries are going to have to modify their way of producing, based on quantity and not specification.

The future is in the creation of personalized products, at the customer's choice, so that he sees himself reflected in his purchase and feels that with her he is different from others. There is talk of the "intelligent industry", one that responds to those needs, that knows what each customer expects and needs at all times. This requires a development of digitalization and data processing in which Blockchain technology becomes more than necessary.

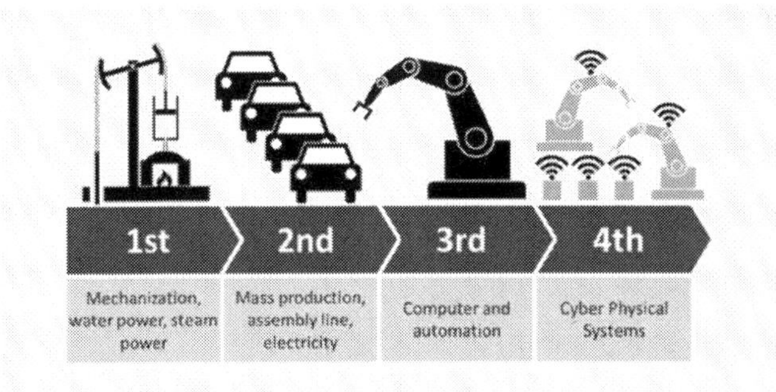

Coinsquare graph showing that cyber systems interacting with physical systems will allow the new industrial leap

Data is increasingly necessary for the success of a business. And if we had a system capable of collecting everything our customers think, analyzing and managing all the information, and telling us just what will succeed because it is precisely what has inferred from the clients' thoughts? Well, that is the task of Big Data, of the internet of things, of these new technologies that require colossal databases, new and with innovative possibilities.

An intelligent industry capable of responding to the needs of each client is necessary. This implies a decentralization of information. Previously, the information was treated so that the mass product responded to most requirements. But now we have to respond to all requests one by one, the clientele has become more diverse and that requires an immediate decentralization of the process of collecting and managing information with commercial power.

Product diversification will lead to diversification in negotiations with suppliers. It will not be enough to have a few in particular, but when manufacturing more diverse products, it will be necessary to contact the more suppliers better, and within them, also with a wide variety of materials and products. Can you imagine having to reach an agreement with each of the one hundred suppliers that you could get to use? And how awkward it would be to contact one of them just because you need a specific material? To all this it tries to solve the broad databases of Blockchain and its smart contracts, which would speed up all this bureaucracy. The agreement would be made by consensus through the automated characteristics of the blockchain in each transaction, avoiding intermediaries and personal agreements. These types of economic networks are called M2M communications.

And how could blockchain improve digital commerce? Here the options are incalculable. In an automated process such as online shopping, the blockchain offers impossible freedom, security and agility without that technology. And in an environment where trust is rather low, since people do not end up trusting online shopping, the consensus of smart contracts through the blockchain could provide that point of trust that is still missing in digital commerce.

Practical exercise 22

Digital platforms such as Amazon or eBay monopolize more and more market rank and threaten to become the destroyers of other companies. Do you think that Blockchain will favor them in this process of market absorption or that it will harm them instead?

Universal data records

Not long ago, all personal data, such as the census of a population, were collected by hand and stored in infinite filing cabinets. Luckily, the digital era brought computers and facilitated the management of this data. Blockchain is a step forward in the management of this type of records.

Wherever a large record of data is necessary, such as the census of a population, marriage, birth or death certificates, work lives ..., Blockchain always has a lot to contribute, especially in the security aspect.

To begin with, the loss of data would be avoided as there are as many copies of the registry as there are strings. These would be unalterable, so it could not be manipulated to benefit particular cases, ending the corruption of the administration. Duplicates would also be avoided. In the same way that the same bitcoin cannot exist twice, neither could an identity; A person could not be registered in several cities at once. Not to mention the consensus rules incorporated in the chain. Democratically, it could be established how this data can be treated and how not. Tierion or Fatcom are companies that already develop this service.

TIERION

Collaborative economy

The collaborative economy allows technology to be used for the benefit of many users. One of the most successful examples in Spain is the BlaBlaCar platform, which puts thousands of users in contact to share a car on their trips, so that the driver gets an economic benefit when filling his vehicle instead of traveling alone and travelers They get to pay less for their trips.

However, such agreements facilitated by digital media always find their obstacles in laws and governments, which see these services more as a way to avoid taxes than as a way of understanding among adults. This platform, in particular, reduces public transport routes, and since they do pay taxes, the rulers will always tend to legislate in their favor.

Today, there are many cases in which governments have enacted laws against this type of collaborative economy initiatives. Another of the most popular cases is that of Uber.

However, the implementation of Blockchain is crucial to determine these personal agreements as independent agreements. Currently, most collaborative economy actions act through a company, such as BlaBlaCar, which is finally the one that receives the legal blows. Instead, acting through the blockchain, in a decentralized manner, would be the perfect way to make these agreements independent interactions, and therefore impossible to prohibit.

Practical exercise 23

Juan wants to publish a book and for this he decides to opt for a collaborative economy method such as crowdfunding. Contact a platform that manages this type of initiatives and this tells you that you have to make a previous report on the project and the chances of success. Once done, the platform tells him that he does not think it could be an interesting project and that they will not risk his time and his means in carrying it out, but that if Juan makes a contribution of € 500, they will allow him to publish it on the web. After the entry, the project begins, but in the middle of this the platform decides to withdraw it because it is not according to the philosophy of the web. After many claims, Juan gets it to be published again and completes it successfully. Once completed, pay the agreed 8% of the collection to the platform.

How do you think Juan's experience would have improved a collaborative economy based on Blockchain?

Digital identity

Today, identifying yourself on the Internet in each service, website or platform is a tedious process. Having to enter the data every time we are going to use a website and remember what password and username we use for each one becomes increasingly cumbersome. And if we use the same data for all, we compromise security.

An alternative to facilitate this whole process is to activate the option of remembering web browser passwords, but that increases the risk that they can supplant us. It would be enough to have access to our device to use our platforms and, in fact, when someone suffers the theft of his mobile, the criminal usually has free access to all his social networks, not to mention banking applications.

Blockchain is offered as an alternative to this entire problem as a fingerprint in the chain that could be used universally in each identification process. It would be something similar to what Facebook does, which allows us to access through its registration a multitude of pages, applications and systems, provided that these have integrated that possibility. But, despite the comfort it provides, we need Facebook as a centralizing element: it is as if we gave you our ID to show it to everyone.

Blockchain offers an independent, universal and secure identification system, with all the authentication algorithms that this technology incorporates. This system is already used by companies such as Onename, Keybase or Shocard.

Shocard is a digital identification unification company

Blockchain for health

The healthcare industry is a clear example of an information disorder. Thousands of centers act differently, use different medications for the same ailments and manage patient data in different ways. Not to mention the experimental world to which they are in constant union and in permanent dependence. Each health center sets its standards, each pharmaceutical brand also, and in the middle of this tug of war, the patient continues to suffer.

Today, it is the social and business factors that move the healthcare universe, and the demands of each other, although perhaps not in the most appropriate direction, make the sector move forward. But more and more, it is the patient who demands. He is no longer an uninformed subject who leaves his health in the hands of doctors, wants to know what happens to him, how he will be treated and what options he has and why he has them. He is aware that what he needs is beyond a simple person dressed in a robe. You need to know what you will be treated with and how it has worked in other patients before, and have the power to decide on your own therapy.

And that, in a centralized sector, is impossible to solve. The patient demands independence, and that is a nuisance to the current system based on "ordering and command" whose only way of functioning is to treat a generalized mass, leaving aside an individualism that would only involve organizational headaches. The system is not enough; it cannot treat each patient exclusively. However, each person, biologically, is by himself, and does not respond like the rest. Something fails. A more open, powerful structure with greater possibilities is needed. And that is where Blockchain, with its ability to automate and relate information beyond what the current system would entail organizational chaos, comes into play.

Blockchain is also the only way to end pharmaceutical fraud and the illegal sale of medicines. If both producers and consumers are included in the chain, all movements will be recorded in this chain and any transaction that does not comply with the consensus rules established in the chain itself cannot be carried out.

Also in the research process, the chain offers numerous advantages, as the Blockchain Health Co. project demonstrates. This platform manages and organizes a large amount of patient data that is extremely useful when investigating a drug. The information is also received in a strictly anonymous and encrypted manner. It is as if a laboratory could access all the data of the disease that it tries to eradicate with the tranquility of the patients to know that their data is being treated anonymously.

BlockchainHealth

Guardtime, with the support of the Estonian government, is a pioneer in the management of clinical records databases through Blockchain. All patients have their history recorded in a chain of blocks that can be accessed by different health centers, so that the tedious bureaucracy of sending documents between different centers ends when there are transfers or a patient decides to change institutions. Recall that Blockchain has a universal character, so that a patient's medical history could be accessed anywhere in the world.

Practical exercise 24

In 2014, England approved the sale of medical records of public hospitals. The VISC + project did the same with Catalan hospitals, making clinical records available to private companies. IDental patients had to be involved in legal proceedings in order to obtain their own history ...

A) Do you think that the sale of medical records under the objective of improving medicines will really benefit patients?

Do you think the individual should be the owner of his medical history and not the center he goes to?

Digital storage

Today we use several different devices (desktop, laptop, mobile, tablets ...) and that in all of them we need to share crucial information, cloud storage systems have become a necessary solution. We can access from the mobile phone in a cafeteria a file that we were using in the morning in the laptop. Dropbox, Sky Drive, Google Drive ... have become work tools.

But imagine what would happen if one day one of those companies decided to close due to lack of liquidity, or simply because they want to devote themselves to more profitable alternatives. If they don't get the expected economic benefit, they won't be working with losses for you. In that case, you would lose all your files stored on your platform. We completely depend on them, their conditions and the way they work.

Blockchain is offered as an alternative by acting not as a storage platform, but as a P2P exchange network. As the blockchain is a complete and immovable record, which retains until the first block, the information would never be lost. Nor would there be the option for an organization to decide to eliminate it: there would be one copy of the chain per user, so that for it to disappear everyone would have to stop using it suddenly, something quite unlikely.

And more important than that, the information would only be accessible to yourself or to those with whom you would like to share it, but there would be no need for it to be stored on a server owned by any entity. The chain is not from anyone and belongs to everyone. That would be the only option that your files could retain true confidentiality. While using current cloud storage systems, your files will always be in the possession of third parties.

This system would also allow costs to be lower. By working through copies on the different nodes, the expense of storage servers, or of the personnel responsible for maintaining the platform, is avoided.

Some companies that already use Blockchain for this purpose are Storj, Datacoin or Factom.

Practical exercise 25

Determine if the following statements are true or false to understand the advantages of blockchain storage:

	T	F
If a traditional cloud storage company closes, I lose the stored data		
If one of the nodes of the Blockchain network goes down, I lose the stored data		
My data stored in traditional services is not accessible to anyone		
My data stored in Blockchain is not accessible to anyone		
Blockchain provides better storage advantages, but the cost is higher		

EXERCISE SOLUTIONS

1

The first scheme corresponds to statement B and the second scheme to statement A.

2

· False: Bitcoin is the first application developed on Blockchain technology.

· False: Bitcoin is not an entity; it is a platform where users can freely exchange without intermediaries.

· True.

· False: Blockchain technology ensures that you accept only one of the two transactions.

· False: the verification is carried out by the users of the chain and not by a centralizing element.

3

A: Anyone can be part of Bitcoin, without prior permission.

B: Once the Bitcoin client is installed, the user makes a copy of the chain on their own device; There is no centralizing server.

C: The chain copy is updated every time someone makes a transaction.

D: It is not necessary to provide personal data.

E: You cannot veto access to any user.

F: All users operate on equal terms, established in the chain's own programming.

G: The verification is carried out by the rest of the users by comparing the copies of their chains.

4

A: It would be impossible to do something like that with bitcoins. From one day to another, Cypriot banks decided to retain their clients' money and keep a percentage of their savings. The blockchain does not have that capacity for decision and maneuver, it is obliged to act as designed and cannot introduce actions such as those from one day to another.

5

· Symmetric cryptography
· Hashing
· Asymmetric cryptography

6

If the miners decrease, the difficulty goes down so that the rest can solve faster and keep the pace of 10 minutes per block.

If the miners increase, the difficulty goes up so that they resolve slower and keep up.

If the mining power increases, the difficulty also increases so that the rhythm is constant.

7

A: No. Miners will continue to receive bonuses in the form of commissions when validating transactions.

B: With the current system, no. An incentive is necessary for miners to recover the expense invested in the need to validate transactions.

C: If someone developed an ultra-efficient technology capable of absorbing 51% of the total world mining power, it could introduce malicious blocks into the chain.

8

A: On the one hand it favors them, since it encourages users to buy and conserve, stimulating the growth of the network. On the other, the more capital conserved, the greater the efficiency of the method, and at the beginning of the currency this is usually rather scarce.

B: In this case it depends on the amount of coins stored, so there is still a numerical competition.

C: An association that collects all the funds from its users would be more likely to receive the rewards. If they exceeded 51% of the total funds, they could even control the blockchain.

9

The statements 2, 4 and 6 are incorrect.

10

In the first case, Juan would have to optimize scalability since it is a worldwide project with a huge number of users and decentralization, so that they can freely establish the conditions of home exchange. It is precisely this great mass of users and the freedom of conditions that would compromise security.

Maria would also need scalability to make exchanges across the planet but would compromise decentralization: she needs to know and control the exchanges to collect her commission. Of course, this vigilance would provide security, provided that Mary was honest.

Roberto does not need scalability since it will be a closed application for the few members of his company, but he will need security so that the sneaks do not extend and reach ears that do not have to arrive and decentralization so that only the interested recipients receive it.

11

	PU	PR	FC
Anyone can access			
Previous permission is			
ID required			
Anonymous participation			
Decentralized algorithms			
Own Algorithms			
Slow transaction			
Fast transaction			

12

A: The bank sacrifices the decentralization capacity since it is interested in exercising authoritarian control over the network. Instead, it takes advantage of the scalability and security features.

B: No, and it is precisely that characteristic that threatens its existence. Banking companies intend to discredit decentralization and base the use of Blockchain trying to justify the need for control, extending the belief of the public blockchain as a chaotic and unsupported environment.

13

A: The risk of not implementing blockchain in the "internet of things" is that the platform could give priority to one information or another depending on its economic benefits, altering the function of collecting and analyzing it. On the other hand, blockchain would act according to the parameters established in the chain itself, without obeying a particular interest and without being able to modify it based on the economic contracts obtained.

14

The contract stipulates that the homebuyer makes a monthly payment. Each month, through an automatic action, the economic transaction from the buyer to the seller would be made. If this is not exercised, a second trigger could automatically activate the change of authorship, becoming the seller of the homeowner once the buyer has breached the payment. All this, without the need for intermediaries, notaries or lawyers. Finally, it would be necessary to incorporate a trigger that terminated the contract once all the relevant payments were made.

15

- Blockchain is responsible for paying the remuneration stipulated in the insurance if any of its specifications are met,· generating absolute trust in the client.

- The automatism of the management generates savings in the cost of personnel.

- The fact of being able to share a database with other companies allows us to be more competitive and not stay behind them.

16

A) The system is similar to hashing, where a function "translates" the original information into an unknown language and decrypts it again before the receiver.

B) With regard to security, creating a private blockchain would allow double shielding in communication. As for decentralization, the message would only be shared between sender and receiver, without a vulnerable central element and eliminating intermediaries vulnerable to corruption. In addition, the fewer elements involved in the communication, the less points of vulnerability.

17

Through other platforms, download data is from the platform itself, which can be altered to reduce payments to the author. On the other hand, through Blockchain an automatic payment can be stipulated for each download, so that it is direct and not made by a third party.

18

The main problem a new telecommunications company faces is infrastructure. It is very high to build a network through which to operate.

If Blockchain strengthens itself as a universal system to avoid protocol interference, a new operator could act on the established blockchain, saving numerous infrastructure costs.

The consumer would benefit as there would be a greater offer of operators and their freedom to choose between them would be greater.

19

One of the biggest limitations when creating a vote is the high cost of its management. This argument justifies that only a few votes are taken every four years, limiting citizen participation. Blockchain would allow voting from home, eliminating all the mobilization of polling stations, security, ballots ... That would allow to open voting processes even for minor issues, by way of specific referendums, and improving citizen participation in essential issues beyond a mere consultation every four years.

20

Yes and the clearest example is Sharge. The company has generated a device capable of creating and sharing energy between individuals. Since this activity is illegal, it has also invented its own currency, so that the energy generated is not "sold", but is rewarded with this token that is acquired in times of leave and then used in times where it is necessary to buy Energy. Thus, the generation and use of energy is freely and spatially regulated.

21

The immovable blockchain registration would also allow knowing at all times when, where and by whom the accesses have been made through this security system. It would be impossible to modify this registry by one person, which makes it difficult for an individual to try to erase their steps.

22

Blockchain will individually improve the large digital companies by increasing their performance at the level of security and data management, but it could be an equalizing element in terms of online sales. The advantage of the big ones like Amazon and eBay are their already established digital platforms, difficult to match for any new company. However, a unified blockchain, which incorporated all the options so that customers could expand their access, would allow any company that wanted it to get in the Blockchain attempt to incorporate all global information in a decentralized way to get into the car. A shared infrastructure would match the opportunities of established and new businesses. And, of course, it will improve the consumer experience, which will have access to more options.

23

In the first place, Juan would have been free to publish his project, without the need for a platform to validate it or request a previous report. He would not have had to depend on his criteria, much less the commission of € 500 for his project to be published. By not depending on a centralizing element such as the platform, nobody could have withdrawn their project in the middle of it, and would not have needed to claim to continue it. Finally, once achieved, the 8% commission of the intermediary platform would also have been saved.

24

A: Sharing medical records among research care centers could be beneficial for the creation and improvement of medications, but this information should be shared anonymously, as Blockchain technology might allow. If made explicitly, many companies could buy the records for non-medical purposes. For example, to decide whether or not to hire a potential worker.

B: The individual should be the sole owner of his medical history. Blockchain could allow it, it would be the individual who decides with which center to share their information, without it having to be stored in any entity or organization.

25

Determine if the following statements are true or false to understand the advantages of blockchain storage:

	T	F
If a traditional cloud storage company closes, I lose the stored data	x	
If one of the nodes of the Blockchain network goes down, I lose the stored data		x

My data stored in traditional services is not accessible to anyone		**x**
My data stored in Blockchain is not accessible to anyone	**x**	
Blockchain provides better storage advantages, but the cost is higher		**x**

Bibliography

AMMOUS, SAIFEDEAN, *"El patrón Bitcoin. La alternativa descentralizada a los bancos centrales"*, Ediciones Deusto, 2018.

—*"Blockchain tecnology: what is it good for?,* Banking & Finance Law Review, vol.33, nº.3, 2018.

ANTONOPOULOS, ANDREAS M., *"Mastering Bitcoin: Programming the Open Blockchain",* O´Reilly, 2017.

— *"Internet del Dinero",* Volumen 1, 2017.

— *"The Internet of Money",* Volumen 2, 2017.

— *"Mastering Ethereum: Building Smart Contracts and DApps",* O´Reilly, 2018.

BARRIO, M., *"Derecho Público e Internet: la actividad administrativa de regulación de la red",* Madrid, Instituto Nacional de Administración Pública, 2017.

BEN ALEXEI., *"Altcoins Book Guide: A Comprehensive Manual on Investing in Alternative Cryptocurrencies*", 2018.

BOAR, ANDREI., *"Descubriendo el Bitcoin: Cómo funciona, cómo comprar, invertir, desinvertir",* Profit Editorial, 2018.

BURNISKE CHRIS y TATAR, JACK., *"Cryptoassets: The innovative investor´s guide to bitcoin and beyond",* McGraw-Hill, 2017.

CHAMPAGNE PHIL y PREUKSCHAT, ALEX., *"El Libro de Satoshi",* 2018.

DOMINGO, CARLOS., *"Todo lo que querías saber sobre bitcoin, criptomonedas y blockchain: y no te atrevías a preguntar",* Ediciones Temas de Hoy, 2018.

DUARTE, EUGENIO, *"Blockchain: La última disrupción en la industria de los servicios financieros",* 2017.

GALINDO, JUAN CARLOS y RAMIREZ, BASILIO., *"Bitcoin: ¿Amenaza u Oportunidad?,"* Círculo Rojo, 2017.

GATES, MARK, *"Cadena de Bloques. La guía para entender todo lo referente a blockchain, el bitcoin, las criptomonedas, los contratos inteligentes y el futuro del dinero",* 2017.

GONZALEZ-MENESES, MANUEL, *"Entender Blockchain. Una introducción a la Tecnología de Registro Distribuido",* Aranzadi, 2017.

GONZÁLEZ OTERO, JUAN MANUEL, *"Bitcoin la moneda del futuro",* Madrid, Unión Editorial, 2013.

IBÁÑEZ JIMÉNEZ, JAVIER WENCESLAO., *"Derecho de Blockchain: y de la tecnología de registros distribuidos",* Aranzadi, 2018.

— *"Blockchain: Primeras cuestiones en el ordenamiento español"*, Editorial Dykinson, 2018.

KELLY BRIAN, *"The Bitcoin Big Bang. How Alternative Currencies Are About to Change the Word"*, Wiley, 2015.

LÓPEZ LÉRIDA, JOAQUÍN y MORA PÉREZ, JOSÉ JUAN., *"La economía de Blockchain: los modelos de negocio de la nueva web"*, 2016.

MÁRQUEZ SOLÍS, SANTIAGO, *"Bitcoin. Guía completa de la moneda del futuro"*, RaMa Editorial, 2016.

— *"Bitcoin. ¿Jaque mate al sistema financiero?*, 2015.

MARTIN FERNANDEZ, J., *"Todo sobre Bitcoin. Aspectos económicos, fiscales, contables y administrativos,* Madrid, Lefebre-El Derecho, 2015.

MOUGAYAR, WILLIAM., *"La Tecnología Blockchain en los negocios. Perspectivas, práctica y aplicación en internet"*, Ediciones Anaya, 2017.

NAKAMOTO, SATOSHI., *"Bitcoin: A Peer-to-Peer Electronic Cash System"*, 2008.

OCARI, B. EMILIANO., *"Blockchain y Smart Contracts. La revolución de la confianza"*, RC Libros, 2018.

PASCUAL MORENO, SONIA., *"Criptotrading, Iniciación al Trading de Criptomonedas"*, 2018.

PASTOR SEMPERE, CARMEN y VILAROIG MOYA, RAMÓN., *"Blockchain: aspectos tecnológicos, empresariales y legales"*, Aranzadi, 2018.

POPPER NATHANIEL., *"Digital Gold: Bitcoin and the inside story of the misfits and millionaires trying to reinvent money"*, Harper Paperbacks, 2016.

PREUKSCHAT, ALEX, *"Blockchain: la revolución industrial de internet,"* Planeta, 2017.

REID, F. and HARRIGAN, M, *"An Analysis of Anonymity in the Bitcoin System"*, 2011.

RIOJA, L., *"La moneda y su historia", Buenos Aires, Editorial Dunken,* 2014.

RIVERS, COLIN y ROJAS, MOISÉS., *"Secretos de las Criptomonedas, Bitcoin. Cómo crear tu propio negocio del bitcoin"*, Ediciones lavdvd.com, 2017.

RYB, ALEJO, *"1 Bitcoin= 1 Millón de dólares"*, 2017.

ROMAN ALEXANDER., *"Ethereum: Manual para invertir, crear y programar la texnología blockchain"*, 2018.

— *"IOTA: Introducción a la tecnología de Tangle"*, 2018.

— *"Ripple y XRP: Manual de monedas XRP y de la tecnología Ripple"*, 2018.

SÁNCHEZ OSCAR, M., *"Bitcoin. Qué son las criptomonedas y cómo ganar dinero con ellas"*, 2017.

SURDA, P., *"Economics of Bitcoin"*, 2011.

TAPSCOTT, DON and ALEX., *"La Revolución Blockchain. Descrubre cómo esta nueva tecnología transformará*

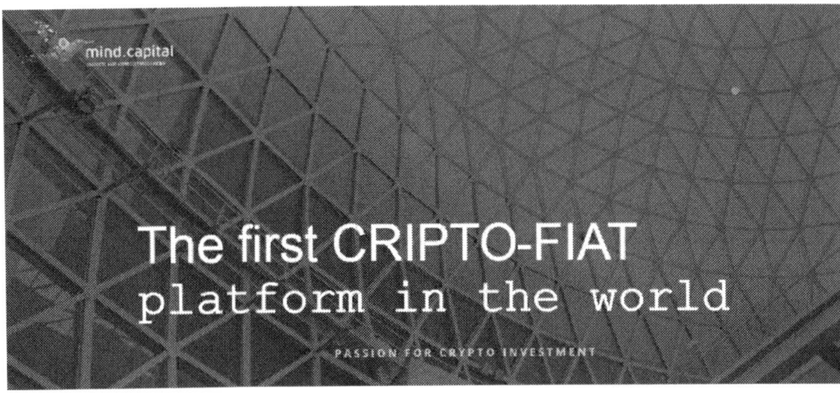

Why do we have a hummingbird in our logo?

The meaning of the symbol of the hummingbird over time reflects our values:

01

Great achievements

Formerly, in many cultures, talismans were carried in the form of hummingbirds, as a symbol of work, as a representation that "A group capable of working in a team will be able to achieve great things "**A group capable of working in a team will be able to achieve great things**".

02

Prosperity

When flying, the infinity symbol can be observed in its movements and it has been given a meaning of prosperity, since it forms this symbol with its wings approximately 50 to 70 times per second. It is said that seeing a hummingbird is a sign of **good luck**.

03

Protection / Security

In time of war it represented protection for warriors. The god of war and the sun, Huitzilopochtli, of the mexica culture, had a hummingbird in his left hand.

Gonzalo
García-Pelayo

Heads mind.capital

Gonzalo García-Pelayo has been a music producer, film director, radio host, television host and is famous for having beaten the casinos in the nineties with his roulette system, the story of which has been shown in movie theaters with the movie «The Pelayos». He has also written several books on betting, «The fabulous story of Los Pelayos», «Learn to play poker with Los Pelayos» y «Bet to win».

In 2006 he opened his school to win at online poker «Los Pelayos Poker» and shortly after, revolutionized the world of sports betting. **Now, he has turned all his experience to find a way to earn money with crypto-assets.**

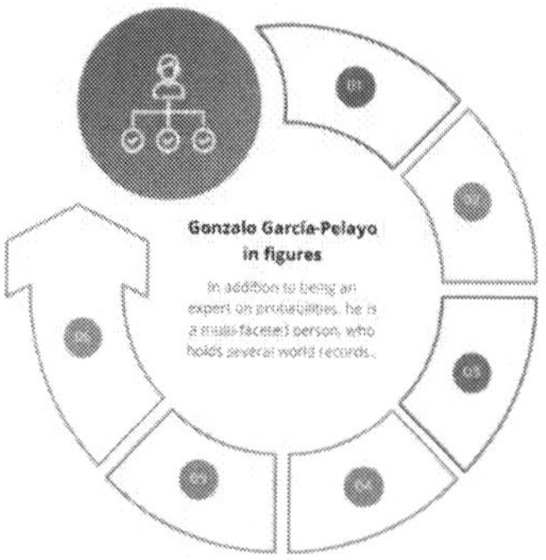

01 He is the person who has won the most money at roulette in the world

02 He is the only person in the world who has developed proven winning systems for casinos, horse races, pools, sports betting and poker

03 He holds the world record in the number of records produced in a year

04 His film "Living in Seville" is considered one of the 100 best Spanish films in history and one of the best 900 worldwide

05 He is one of the few Spaniards who has appeared on the cover of Le Monde

06 He has directed 14 films and has produced more than 160 albums and is known as one of the fathers of Andalusian rock

¿How does it work?

Profitability is our priority

The technology developed by mind.capital allows us to **study the evolution of the main crypto-assets and their price in different currencies** and operate in the market by using advanced algorithms. After years of research, we have optimized the system to obtain maximum profitability.

Real-time monitoring and analysis of the main crypto-assets and their price in different currencies

AI algorithms developed to find buying/selling opportunities

Optimization and continuous adaptation of the platform

The system in action

We like things to be clear

From your control panel at any time you can **see in real-time how our Artificial Intelligence algorithms** work finding investment opportunities and the profitability obtained in each operation performed.

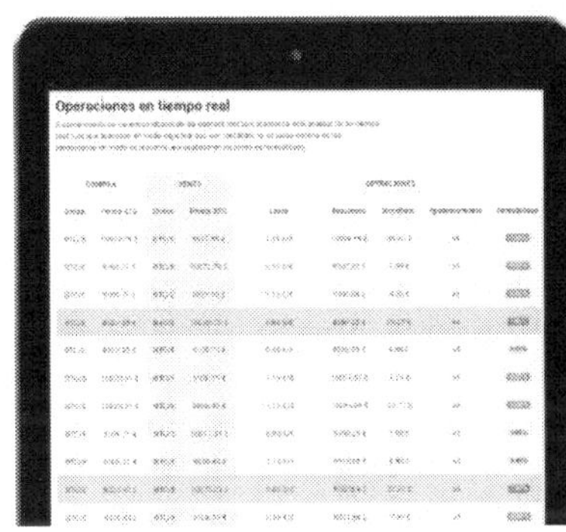

Blockchain integrated

Having **blockchain** integrated **ensures** that the money you have in your account is really within the platform and **just one click away from your wallet**.

What do we offer?

Profitability
The entire system is implemented to optimize performance and profitability.

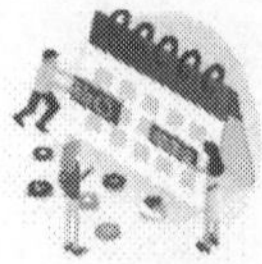

Daily settlement
Every day, the platform distributes the profitability obtained the previous day. Every working day you will have the profits obtained in your account.

Liquidity
You can request the recovery of the contribution after the end of the investment term.

Blockchain
The entire platform is integrated with Blockchain, so both payments and withdrawals are made automatically and in a few minutes.

Ease of use
Contributions can be made with both BTCs and credit card.

Technology
Years of research and development (R&D) and the latest technology for the benefit of the investor.

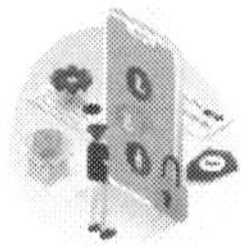

Available for anyone
Any person, from $ 100, can participate in the profitability, experience and technology developed by mind.capital.

Team
In addition to Gonzalo García-Pelayo, there is an international team of experts in mathematics, investments and technology behind the mind.capital.

Historical profitability

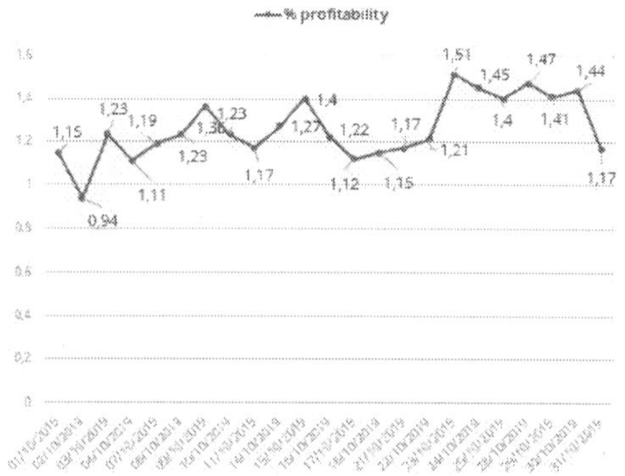

In the latest reports mind.capital is producing a daily return of between 0.5 and 1.5%.

Distribution of profits

Every day, the platform distributes the benefits obtained the previous day
Every day the profits obtained the previous day are distributed among the participants, of which mind.capital retains 35% in management and maintenance expenses.

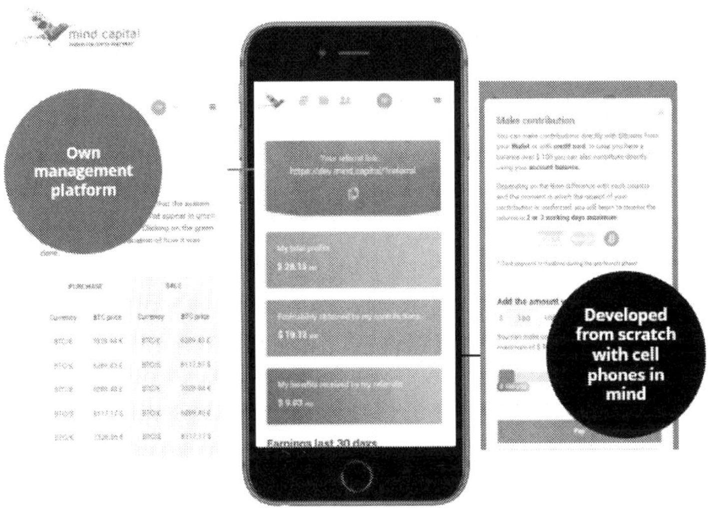

How can I participate?

01

Create an account

To register you only need to fill in the registration form and by providing the code of your referral the registration is **free**.

02

Select the amount

Once inside your administration panel, click on make a contribution and select the amount between $ 100 and $ 100,000.

03

Start making profits

From the first moment you will begin to receive daily in your account the part that corresponds to you from the profitability obtained by the system the previous day.

RoadMap

Our main milestones

The beginnings

Gonzalo García-Pelayo began to be interested in the peculiarities of cryptocurrencies and began to research ways to obtain profitability

The inefficiencies

After several months of research and tests, Gonzalo discovered that there are inefficiencies between cryptocurrency markets and currencies

International experts

He started working on his system with mathematical experts, engineers and analysts from different countries to develop algorithms and software to exploit the inefficiencies found

mind.capital

After more than a year of development, tests and proven profits, now everything is ready to create a platform that allows the system to be brought closer to everyone meaning that anyone can invest.

Development of the platform

An American company specialized in Blockchain is hired to develop mind.capital

Blockchain

Mind.capital is integrated with blockchain. The first tests of investments and automatic withdrawals are made using this technology

Demonstration in real time

The platform is perfected so that some of the operations performed by the system can be seen in real time

Pre-launch

Pre-launch of the platform for experts and large investors

inversores

Madrid

Opening of offices in Madrid

Launch

Launch of the platform for the public

PASSION FOR CRYPTO INVESTMENT

Scams and Ponzi schemes

Due to the cryptocurrency boom, more and more scams and fraudulent projects are emerging. The difference between a scam and a real project is the information that is offered, the generation of value and the proven facts.

mind.capital is a serious investment system which has been developed over several years, which has a team of recognized professionals and only receives income when it obtains profits.

01 Real value

Most cryptocurrencies do not create real value. mind.capital generates value by assuming positions in the crypto-asset market, and so that there are no doubts, what is generated is distributed daily.

02 Fake ICOs

Most scams are fake ICOs. mind.capital is not an ICO, rather, it is a platform that invests in crypto-assets following a developed and tested system.

03 Who is behind them

Fraudulent projects either do not tell you who is behind them or they place little known people at the forefront who then disappear. In mind.capital, **Gonzalo García-Pelayo**, who is widely known in the world of music, film and probabilities, leads the project together with a large team of developers.

04 Pyramids or Ponzi schemes

In these systems the payments of the returns come from the money of the new investors. mind.capital in no case uses percentages of contributions for the payment of the referral system. The payment of the daily returns comes exclusively from the benefits and the platform is economically supported by withdrawing 35% of the returns generated.

Printed in Poland
by Amazon Fulfillment
Poland Sp. z o.o., Wrocław

52668087R00065